D0850139

PAY-OFF

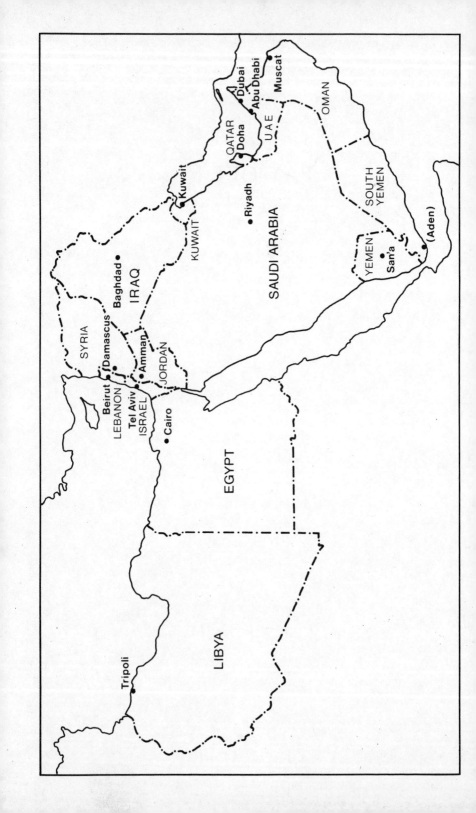

PAY-OFF

*Wheeling and Dealing in
the Arab World*

SAID K. ABURISH

ANDRE DEUTSCH

Appropriately and humbly to my father

First published 1985 by
André Deutsch Limited
105 Great Russell Street London WC1

British Library Cataloguing in Publication Data
Aburish, Said K.
  Pay-off: the world of the Arab intermediary.
  1. Business enterprises – Near East
  2. Brokers in public contracts
  I. Title
  338.6   HF5349.N/

ISBN 0–233–97779–1

Typeset by Inforum Ltd, Portsmouth
Printed in Great Britain by
Ebenezer Baylis & Son Ltd, Worcester

CONTENTS

The governments, having lost their balance, are frightened, intimidated and thrown into confusion by the cries of the intermediary class of society, which, placed between the Kings and their subjects, breaks the sceptre of the monarchs and usurps the cry of the people.

Metternich to the Tsar, 1820

ACKNOWLEDGEMENTS

This list cannot be complete. Thanks are owed to a great number of people who were generous with their time and counsel.

Margaret Hunter and Heather Lakin typed and re-typed the manuscript with all the changes and amendments. They deserve special thanks. My friend, Peter Hopkins, was present at the creation. His gentle persuasion as to my approach to this subject deserves special mention. My wife, Kate, suffered all the tensions which went with finalising the book stoically and offered invaluable advice. My editor at André Deutsch, Sheila McIlwraith, and my agent George Greenfield, nursed my final draft with loving care.

Lastly, during the final phases of writing the book I suffered an almost fatal accident. My good friend Michael McHugh happened to be there, administered first aid and saved my life. My gratitude to him knows no bounds.

INTRODUCTION

I was born into a semi-Bedouin society in the small biblical village of Bethany, outside Jerusalem. It was an entirely Arab society, and I was brought up with the same mores and manners as were the Arabs who became oil-rich and who are the subject of this book.

The journey from Bethany to London, where I now live, has taken forty-nine years, and has involved a complete change in attitude and lifestyle. My education included nine years at local schools, the American University of Beirut and the University of Chicago. I have been, among other things, a reporter for Radio Free Europe, a salesman for Massey Ferguson tractors and senior vice-president of an international advertising agency. I have for twelve years consulted on Middle East business, working for large international corporations, for the Iraqi Government and for an assortment of Middle East governments and businesses.

I know the Arabs and I know the corporations that deal with them. I was, and am, in the middle, both culturally and as a businessman.

This book will offend many people and it isn't likely to make me rich. In having it published I am exposing myself to dangers which range from my position as a consultant on Middle East business being damaged, to being killed by someone who thinks I'm divulging too much. I have neither a death wish nor a pressing need for whatever money the book may earn. So why did I write it?

There are two reasons. First, the abuse of wealth and power in the Middle East has gone too far. Someone, somewhere has to object, to protest, to point the finger. This abuse of wealth, and the debasement of cultural and human values, are nowhere more apparent than in the conduct of business; and business is made possible in the Middle East by the presence of intermediaries. This book is about the intermediary.

Inevitably, the finger will point not only to the Arabs, but to the West as well. Too many Westerners genuinely believe that bribery and corruption in business are a thing of the East. How then do they suppose deals are done across the East/West divide? I hope this book will open their eyes a little.

I am addressing myself to one narrow aspect of the much larger problem of the degeneracy of the social system in today's Middle East. But it is one of the ugliest aspects of what has happened there. And it has been misreported and misunderstood. I feel it is my Arab and human duty to spotlight abuse, and to try to contribute to a better understanding between the lands of my roots and those of my adopted culture.

Said K. Aburish
London, 1984

I

What Is an Intermediary?

Who and what is an intermediary? What does he do? Where and how does he do it? The vague image of the Arab 'fixer' advanced by the Western press, the jet-setting international smoothie who makes a lot of money, is part of the truth. But the answers to these questions are not simple.

In the Middle East today, the intermediary plays a vital role in business dealings. Fundamentally, he is someone who can help a foreign corporation obtain a piece of business in this lucrative, oil-rich market. His help consists of providing the company with an advantage over its competitors by securing the co-operation of someone in power, or with power and influence, to promote its interests. In other words, an intermediary is a person who gets an Arab chief (king, president, sheikh, minister, general, or a relative of theirs) to favour one company's interests over others in return for a commission/bribe which is shared by the intermediary and his political mentor.

With a few exceptions, the Middle East intermediary is an Arab. Occasionally, he is a non-Arab exceptionally knowledgeable in Arab ways and thinking. In either case, he must first ally himself to an Arab chief, one who knows of contracts – particularly big government contracts – as they come up for tender, and can influence how they will be awarded. Having established himself in the confidence of such a chief, the intermediary then looks to match companies with contracts. He must secure the co-operation of the appropriate corporation, and further its cause, while agreeing the best possible percentage of the value of the contract for himself and his mentor.

Present-day Arab chiefs instinctively view their powers and position seriously. They are unlikely to use them except in support of people they trust and with whom they are comfortable. Their inclination to use fellow Arabs as intermediaries is perfectly natural. Members of any nation feel more able to communicate with their compatriots than with foreigners, even when the language is similar (*viz* Britons and Americans). But the Middle East has particularly distinctive ways of thinking, speaking and behaving which Arabs (myself included) tend to feel only Arabs can fully understand.

The Middle East, our territory, is a land which has been shocked into joining the twentieth century by the accident of huge oil wealth. This unprecedented historical circumstance forced the Arabs of Saudi Arabia, Kuwait, Iraq, Qatar, the United Arab Emirates and even Oman to rush into false modernity, and disrupted their traditional way of life. Moreover, oil wealth immediately transformed these countries into important markets for Japanese TV sets, American cars, Swiss watches, French perfumes, British contractors, Thai silks and all the rest. The other countries of the Arab Middle East, Egypt, Jordan, Syria and Yemen benefited indirectly. Though they had little or no oil, they were at the receiving end of generous aid programmes and their doctors, teachers, engineers and lawyers emigrated to the oil-rich countries in thousands, in pursuit of higher salaries and easier lives.

So the whole Arab Middle East came of age with all the symptoms of change and uncertainty; it became a blazing torch towards which international traders trekked. Businessmen of every race and colour rushed to the Middle East to claim a piece of the oil-wealth pie. Their unpreparedness and ignorance showed. They slept in taxis because there were no hotel rooms to be had. They arrived without essential entry visas. They tried to sell beer where Islamic laws forbade it. Recognising their disadvantages, they sought – wisely or foolishly, methodically or without prior planning – for someone to help them with their Middle Eastern business. What they wanted were intermediaries, people who knew the area and were connected with a government authority prepared to promote their companies, their products and services.

What Is an Intermediary?

This began in the early Seventies when the massive increase in oil prices gave the words 'Middle East' and 'Arab' a new and special connotation in countries as distant as Taiwan and Brazil. Of course, intermediaries existed before then, but they were fewer and the sums of money involved were much, much smaller. Besides, until then other parts of the world such as South America were wealthier and came first.

The numbers and status of intermediaries rose against this background. By the mid-Seventies, practically every major company had someone promoting its interests in every Middle Eastern country. Occasionally, an intermediary is astute enough to operate in more than one country, by endearing himself to more than one powerful person. This happens rarely, because the business is demanding, and because benefactors do not relish 'sharing' their intermediaries, due to the delicate nature of the business and the secrecy involved.

The strangeness of the Middle East and its sudden importance for international business made the use of an intermediary necessary. The atmosphere in which he works is unlike any other big business ambience, partly due to the unique kind of competition involved. For example, suppose company X is using an intermediary to promote its chances of winning a sewage contract in Saudi Arabia. The intermediary's source of power is his relationship with a member of the Saudi Royal Family, a prince. Company Y is using another intermediary who is using another prince. So the competition is between one prince and another. Often it is between a prince and a minister, a minister and a minister, and so on in all the variations.

Is intermediary activity pure corruption, to be condemned? To the Arab it is a perfectly acceptable part of business life, an extention of his traditional attitude to money, to giving and receiving. To the strict business ethos of the West it would appear to be bribery, plain and simple. Yet both sides play the game.

How the game is played is another matter. Tactics vary with every deal, and the rules are dictated by, for example, the size and nature of the contract, and the company – its product, its expertise, its national origin. Standards of decent dealing still exist, in this perhaps dubious world, to be upheld or ignored.

The intermediary's relationship with his Arab master is primarily a business one. He is the expert on the international body corporate, who not only produces the right company for the right job, but secures an agreement from that company, and vouches for its reliability to honour the agreement, and to treat the whole deal with confidentiality. He is the hard-hearted charmer who entices corporations into signing away small percentages which eventually become big money – from 2% of $1,000,000 to 4.5% of $11,000,000,000.

There is also a personal element in this relationship, however. The intermediary is the discreet keeper of his master's secrets. Saudi super-intermediary Adnan Khashoggi assumed responsibility for all the Saudi misdeeds connected with the notorious Lockheed scandal. He protected his royal mentors. This endeared him to them and, rather than having a damaging effect, the scandal elevated him and made him their tried and loyal associate.

An intermediary also contends with the petty day-to-day requirements of his mentor/benefactor, which vary according to the latter's tastes. Such services may include buying cars with gold doorhandles, arranging secluded holidays in exotic places and procuring ladies of pleasure.

The prince, sheikh or minister relies upon his intermediary to interpret the unfamiliar world of the twentieth century for him. This interpretation is guided by the intermediary's singular interest in money.

In dealing with a company, the second part of the equation, the intermediary assumes the mantle of the sophisticated international businessman with special knowledge of how big Middle East contracts are won and lost. In cases where laws and regulations forbid a company to pay off or bribe an intermediary and his chief, schemes must be devised to circumvent such laws. Because US Government laws forbid paying a bribe or anything resembling a bribe, the intermediary and company call such payments consultancy fees. When West German laws forbid the sale of arms to Iraq, intermediaries dealing with German arms manufacturers prepare paperwork showing the arms to be destined to another country, and either divert them en route or reship them when they get there.

The intermediary has to transmit confidence, to convince the company that he and his master are the best chief/intermediary team to serve its interests. There will be examples of how that is done, and indeed undone, throughout this book, but it is worthwhile stating clearly that peddling the intangibles of power and influence is one of the most demanding sales jobs ever known.

The lifestyle of the intermediary is fairly accurately described in newspapers and magazines. He is high spending, globetrotting, girl chasing and closer to a real-life James Bond than real spies (they tend to hide things). The flashy exterior is there, and so is the gold and the guns and the people who can and do use them.

Every intermediary must speak good English, the language of international business. Expertise in other languages besides Arabic, particularly French, adds to the glitter. He must know the right hotels (George V in Paris, Savoy in London, Pierre in New York), discos (Annabel's in London, Régine's in Paris and New York), casinos (tens) and nightclubs (hundreds). He must be au fait with fashion (Dior, Gucci), expensive cars (Rolls-Royces, Lamborghinis), Havana cigars (Monte Cristo) and drink (Black Label whisky, Cristel and Dom Perignon champagne).

Contrary to popular opinion, regular whorehouses are not good enough for them. Escort services, airline hostesses, housewives in need of extra cash and even night-club girls are preferred. And there is a whole breed of dumb blonde without specific roots who refers to Cannes as cans, Arabs as Ay-rabs, pronounces the Middle Eastern name Manir as Manure, and who always manages to have a sick mother, father or even child who needs expensive medical care.

What sort of people become intermediaries? Where do they come from, and what qualifies them to perform this elusive function which involves diplomacy, wealth and occasionally danger and death? They are usually Arabs, and they love money; beyond that they have little in common. Respectable businessmen have become intermediaries, seeing it as an easier, faster way to amass wealth. Doctors work themselves into the confidence of important patients and become intermediaries. Journalists impress a potentate with their worldly knowledge, pimps discard the limitations of their unwholesome job, and opt for intermediary work. Even drivers for important people work themselves into it.

There is no specific preparation for the job, but this doesn't mean that perceived competence is enough, or that there is no hierarchy or class system within this Mafia-like fraternity; quite the opposite. As with most class systems, two things are important: money and family background. In this business, someone with background and money is ahead of someone with money alone. You can do without the family connections, however – not without money.

The intermediary is a lavish spender, for several reasons. Celebrating money is a Koranic command (Thou shalt speak of the bounty of thine Maker), and flaunting money is a reflection of the hedonistic Middle Eastern attitude to which Christians as well as Moslems subscribe. He must appear wealthy to keep his standing with fellow intermediaries and with companies. Money is the measure of his success, lack of it the mark of failure. Since the business doesn't allow for trust, respect, or other rewards, spending heavily is the most obvious way to impress people.

An intermediary operating in Iraq may need the help of another working in Oman, because the latter is close to a certain company. His chances of soliciting his colleague's help depend on his reputation, which is made of money. To the companies, appearing successful means being successful, and signifies an acceptable track record.

Companies have very often asked my advice about fellow intermediaries in countries outside my network. As a recommendation, I might say, 'He must be doing all right, he just bought a big house in the south of France,' or 'He just pulled off a goodie – he's in fine shape.' Disparaging descriptions can be equally exaggerated and sink as low as, 'He's a small-timer, never handled anything over $100,000,' or 'His bill at Régine's goes back two years.'

Communications operate by word of mouth, and one has to learn to distinguish between rumour and fact. This requires keeping track of the intermediary family and the business they do.

Someone trying to impress me told me shamelessly that he had concluded a deal I had done myself. He was seeking my co-operation on another matter; he walked out empty-handed.

Loud, vulgar money works; the house in the south of France, the Mercedes sports car, the club memberships, the names of the Savile Row tailor and French tie maker. Then there is the £5 tip to the hotel doorman, and the daily visit to the barber for a wash and blow dry.

As far as family background is concerned, the intermediary is most often a non-desert Arab, from a country without oil; a Lebanese, Palestinian, Syrian or Egyptian. Such people are better educated to deal with international corporations than their desert neighbours, but they are still Arabs, able to communicate with and befriend the decision makers.

The oil-rich Arabs control the purse strings, but they have an inferiority complex regarding the more advanced, though poor, Lebanese, etc., and get a kick out of hiring members of these countries' established aristocracies to work for them. Some people have become name salesmen, using their family's reputation to approach both the Arab chief and the company. The Lebanese have an offensive habit of stating, 'I come from a good family.' A Kuwaiti or Saudi chief attaches considerable importance to the family background of his intermediary. It is both a source of personal gratification to have a 'name' person work for him, and a reflection of a genuine belief that a 'name' Arab is more competent than an ordinary one. A Saudi sheikh told me no less than twenty times that his intermediary was the son of an Egyptian pasha (lord). Another pointed proudly to his subordinate and whispered to me that he was a descendant of the Prophet. A third kept mumbling that his intermediary was a member of the Lebanese parliament.

In fact, to the Arab chief an ordinary Arab is not only inferior to a 'name' Arab, he is less attractive than an ordinary Western person. Hiring a Westerner may cause language difficulties, but if that is not an obstacle, then it is as good for the ego as hiring a name Arab. After all, it isn't such a long time ago that the Sheikh of Sharja, Ahmad Al Kassemi, was a truck driver in the British Army. This reducing of former masters or superiors to sidekicks is a totally understandable psychological phenomenon, be they name

7

Arabs or former British Army officers; American or Canadian oil men; or French gun-runners.

One of the most unattractive groups within the intermediary world are the stuttering, stammering former majors and colonels of Her Majesty's armed forces. They are militaristic in their obedience, but harbour disdain for their new masters. They hate their jobs, whine about the good old days, and one thanks heaven they are a disappearing breed.

Oil men are often used as intermediaries in deals which have no direct relationship to oil. To the Arab chief, oil is money, and anyone who understands oil can make money regardless of his capabilities. The head of a small public Canadian oil company found himself requested to buy light arms for a sheikh from the United Arab Emirates. As he knew nothing about it he hired former SAS chief Bill Sterling who did the job for him.

Questionable characters with a French background have their attraction. In addition to their Gallic élan, they have a built-in Mediterranean naughtiness which works. They come across as being able to outsmart opponents. One of them offered a non-existent cache of 105mm ammunition both to Iraq and to its enemy-at-war Iran. When each expressed interest he wouldn't move until Iraq made a down payment, enough for him to retire to Guadaloupe on.

But a large majority of intermediaries come from the four non-desert Arab countries, and rivalry is rife among the nationalities. The Palestinians loathe the Lebanese, considering them sticky-fingered Phoenician traders, not to be trusted. Of course, the Lebanese hate and despise the Palestinians, and they accuse each other of atrocious social crimes. Palestinians claim superiority in English, for the second language in Lebanon is French. They unite, however, in looking down on the Eygptians and Syrians, as being less educated in Western business ways. Members of a national group tend to favour their own; as the Palestinians say, 'If we don't help each other no one will help us.' Among the Lebanese, solidarity between intermediaries often breaks down according to their religious affiliation; shiites support shiites, Maronites support Maronites, and so on.

They call each other Palestinian or Lebanese 'Mafia', and insult one another readily, sometimes with amusing crudity. Their jibes are calculated to appeal to their masters from the Arabian peninsula. I remember one Palestinian, whose turf was being encroached upon by a Lebanese, looking his macho chief in the eye and informing him that the Lebanese's penis was so small, 'I wouldn't sneeze if he stuck it in my nose.' This earned him howls of laughter, and obliterated the chances of the diminished Lebanese.

An intermediary's status, obviously, hinges on the status of his chief, the solidity of their relationship, the length of time he has been in the business and his personal social qualities in terms of how well he gets around. As we have seen, it depends on the amount of money he makes, and is seen to have, and, to a certain extent, on his family background. Proven business efficiency, as demonstrated, for example, in following up on projects and keeping clients informed, is not considered a major attribute within the intermediary club and therefore does not contribute to one's standing.

A corporation may very well value such competence, as well as language proficiency and one's ability to judge a situation. But it is the people in the Middle East – the master, the fellow intermediaries – who assign one's status; the judgements of the companies are secondary. In some countries, my own firm's standing is much higher with corporations than with our associates because I am not a name Arab, don't have lots of money and am considered difficult, as I refuse to entertain or to frequent gambling casinos and don't share their sense of humour. This has cost me dearly.

Understanding the complex class system inherent in this is something that eludes most representatives of Western corporations. Differentiating between small-timers and successful intermediaries is the same as differentiating between small sheikhs and big sheikhs – it goes below the surface and requires knowledge of the terrain. And the ability to differentiate is vital, for to trade successfully in the Middle East you must know whom to deal with.

I trust that what I mean by the word intermediary is by now clear.

The literal sense, of middleman, go-between, falls short of my meaning. Euphemisms, used by those inside the business, and uncomplimentary alternatives, used by those outside it, are legion. Forms of address, and respect accorded in conversation, are important in the Middle East, so it is interesting to look at the language used in connection with intermediary work.

Intermediaries describe themselves to non-Middle East corporations in various ways. The French-speaking Lebanese insists on using the French 'intermédiaire'. It has an elegant, international, man-of-the-world ring to it and is not harsh like its English counterpart. It fits him perfectly.

Another practitioner, a Harvard-educated Palestinian, assumes a totally haughty air directed at Anglo-Saxon businessmen and refers to himself as a 'functional consultant'. This is supposed to elevate him above those who advise, to the role of doer, one who performs.

When intermediaries call themselves promoters, we are closer to the heart of the matter, though they seldom use the word by itself. Wanting to take the sting out of it, to make it respectable, they talk of business promotion and company promotion, go as far as deal promotion, and I guess they feel better for it.

My personal approach, circuitous but successful, was to describe my company as trying to instil method into a fundamentally entrepreneurial function. I would quickly add that our commissions were modest, reflecting our businesslike attitude. Unlike some other Arabs, I maintained, we were good communicators and meticulously followed up on all projects. This overcame several fears, while indicating a lack of greed and a sense of organisation.

The world is cruel when it comes to describing the intermediary. Even the company people and the Arab chiefs tend to look down on him. Average outsiders view him and his job with considerable and confused misgivings.

Wheeler-dealer is a term often used by the public, but it is a dull, old-fashioned name and is too general. Fixer is fairly accurate, but it emphasises shady happenings. Phrases such as 'he deals in the Middle East', 'he is an Arab Mr Fix-it' and 'he represents Middle East interests' are usefully vague for speakers who like to keep their distance.

Executives in companies using intermediaries are especially cutting about their particular contact. Their language is elaborate; they have firsthand knowledge of the creature and tend to envy the big money he makes. They consider him an unnecessary evil, and this feeling extends to his Arab master, so they speak of 'Prince Abdullah's henchman' or 'Prince Abdullah's sidekick'. But they often descend to 'Prince Abdullah's pimp' or the racially provocative 'Abdullah's Lebanese grocer' or 'Abdullah's PLO stooge'.

The suave, elegant, know-it-all 'intermédiaire' gets it from everyone. Even his Arab master, be he King, president, sheikh, minister, general, or whatever, doesn't respect him. For one thing, traditional Arab niceties of affixing Brother, or Maître, before first names are dispensed with. Then he is reduced to 'my leg man in London' when he is away and 'my man here' when he is present; even more insulting, 'he deals for me, he is Lebanese'. Seldom if ever does he earn the term 'business associate' or 'manager' or anything so polite. When speaking to the company, his Arab master often lowers his associate to 'messenger'.

To be fair, the intermediary gives as good as he gets. There is no love lost. True, in straightforward situations he will refer to his Middle East patron as the 'big man' or the Prince or the Sheikh. These are simple covers to maintain discretion and avoid using the actual name of the man in power. But in private the intermediary can be totally crude. The most common appellation for a master is 'the beast' (*Al Wahash*); others are 'death face', facetiously 'the pretty one', and 'the monster'. Because of his disgusting habit of playing with his nose in public, one master earned the epithet of 'champion nose picker of Saudi Arabia'. These insults are the intermediary's ego-restorers and are used with relish to describe the less civilised man who employs him. They are indicative of the attitude of the Palestinian, Lebanese, Syrian and Egyptian intermediaries towards their desert-folk masters.

The intermediary's references to company people are no more polished than those to his Arab boss. Because the companies he deals with are for the most part capital goods corporations, members of their management tend to be down-to-earth, matter-of-fact people from the Midlands in the UK, the Middle West in America, and so on. These people don't have the varnish of the intermediary, and he usually calls them fallahean – peasants. If he knows his British and American dialects he might go to 'scrubber' for a Brit, 'Okie' for an American and 'wetback' for a Latin.

On the subject of names and definitions, let me introduce the skimmer. Of all the people involved in pay-offs, he is the most truly frightening. An elusive, super-influential character, he can stop a deal in the making unless his demands are met. He is a big-time blackmailer, a top decision-maker in the country where a contract is supposed to take place. He is the one who gets paid no matter who gets the deal, as all intermediaries are at his mercy.

Most of the time the skimmer is more highly placed than the intermediary's boss; occasionally he (or she) is a stubborn equal. In rare instances he is a gutsy bureaucrat, head of a technical committee evaluating a product or project – water treatment plant, bullet-proof vests, school toys, whatever – and he just refuses to use that stamp of approval unless he becomes part of the pay-off equation. This troublesome figure's success or failure depends on the power of the intermediary to circumvent him.

The Arab chief and the company loathe the skimmer. He is the 'skunk', 'hyena' and 'bloodsucker'. He is even more callous than they are and his demands have been known to amount to 70% of all commissions. This happens when he is essential to a deal and secure in his ability to stop it going through; when he is, for example, a director of procurement or a secure minister – when he is simply more important than the chief.

The name-calling and exaggerations common to intermediary activity are part of a disease that has worked itself into the Middle Eastern social system as a whole, the result of the corruption of money.

The old standards have crumbled and sheikh, a tribal chief, is now merely a polite way of addressing a man with money and is no longer the inherited title it once was. Real sheikhs, insisting on remaining apart, have elevated themselves to emirs (princes) and some emirs have elevated themselves into holiness and now call themselves sherrif (descendant of the Prophet). Within all of this, there are big and little sheikhs and emirs though sherrifs are supposedly all the same in the eyes of Allah.

But the word and name game goes beyond what people call themselves and each other. There is a whole separate language and communications system, which extends to inventing elementary code systems for sensitive situations. Here is one we used when involved in a major arms deal with British Aircraft Corporation:

Kite	Plane
Car	Jaguar Fighter Bomber
Garage	Airfield
Car Salesman	BAC Director
Better Associates	British Aircraft Corporation
Arab Friends	Iraqi Air Force
Connoisseur	Chief of Staff
Scouts	Army
ISF	Iraqi Sea Forces
My People	US Government
Frogs	French
First Essential Elements	Commission/Fee Agreement

This was developed for telex and telephone use. One day we sent a message enquiring whether the airfields the Iraqis wished to build were for day flights only or for night-time use also. My secretary made a typographical error and the question went out, 'Should garage accommodate sleeping kikes?' The answer came back an hour later, 'Yah, Man, Yah.'

Linguistic tresspasses, exaggerations, funnies and euphemisms permeate the whole business. They do so in every service business but in this one they are supreme.

For example, the Chief and his sidekick exaggerate the worth and experience of any company with which they work. The wise ones limit the adjectives to the company's quality of performance but others, less careful, exaggerate actual facts and figures and, when exposed, do the company more harm than good. A company with civil contracting experience can, according to them, 'build anything'. Another doing $1,000,000,000 of annual business is 'as big as General Motors'. Someone described a small, Sheffield, private commodities company he represents as 'the largest privately held company in the world but we can't give the exact figures, they are top secret.'

When trying to induce the company to work with him, the intermediary exaggerates the worth and importance of his master. If he is one of the five thousand Saudi princes, then he is 'a favourite of his Uncle, the King', or 'one of the up and coming members of the family' or 'Yamani's right-hand man', or lately 'unlike the rest of his lazy family he is a businessman.'

Something akin to all of this happens within the corporation. Here the company officer tries to sell his board of decision-makers on working with someone. I do not know the method used, except from my experience of cases when we won over a company officer by offering him a slice of the pie. In such cases you have to write the script for him which sometimes backfires. Someone committed to us, a company's Middle East manager, gave us a glowing testimonial, saying our business association in Qatar dated back to 1913. This provoked a board member's sarcastic retort of, 'Yes, they were well known pearl smugglers.' In 1913 that was practically Kuwait's only business.

Invariably, this unreal world full of lies, pretence and buzz words, foreign to ordinary, decent people, is also full of funny stories. Here are my favourite three stories on the subject of names and labels and the confusion they can produce.

A limping Saudi businessman explained his condition to a visitor by stating that he dropped a hammer on his 'foot fingers'. His visitor, a pompous Englishman, kept correcting him, 'I am sure you mean your toes.' 'No, no,' protested the Saudi, 'it is my foot fingers.' Eventually the Englishman prevailed, identifying the appendages on one's feet as toes. The bewildered Saudi refused to lose graciously, 'You Brits complicate everything. Why invent toes when fingers are enough. It is like a contract with a British company. Too many words.'

The second one originated with a company. Their representative who visited me to explore possible 'co-operation' wrote to his managing director referring to me as a 'Lebanese grocer' but suggesting I be contacted nevertheless. The managing director wrote to me enclosing a copy of the internal memorandum by mistake. I sent it back putting 'Palestinian' in place of Lebanese.

The third story has to do with using the telex machine. Unlike the Jews, the Arabs name a man after his eldest son rather than his father; Abu Abdullah means father of Abdullah and Abu Sami,

14

father of Sami — and so on down the line. This is a traditional source of pride in this male-orientated society. It is even impolite to address a man by his first name after he has a son.

Inevitably first names become family names and thus a great many Arab families names begin with Abu.

My name begins with Abu and when I first started in the intermediary business I formed a partnership in London with an Englishman by the name of James. The answerback on our telex machine was Abujam.

When I went to visit a business associate in Jordan, the hospitable Jordanian sent one of his employees to pick me up at the airport. All this employee knew about me was gleaned from our telex correspondence. Because of this, the effusive greeter shook me by the hand constantly referring to me as Abu Jam (father of Jam) and enquiring about the health and well-being of my family, particularly number-one son Jam. Rather than disappoint him, I created a Jam, gave him an age and school and the rest of the sticky details!

2

---•••---

Doing Business in the Middle East

The Middle East, even when we limit it to the Arab Middle East, comprises an area larger than the United States of America. Within it are Egypt and the Sudan, Saudi Arabia and the other countries of the Arabian peninsula, Iraq, Syria, Lebanon and Libya.

Believers in Arabism and mostly Moslem, the inhabitants of this area have common cultural characteristics, as well as indigenous ones which vary considerably from country to country. Some of the differences have historical foundations while others are recent, brought about by colonialists' desires to divide and rule, or the selfish motivation of a king or president bent on protecting himself by promoting his brand of narrow nationalism against the threat of Arab unity or Islamic fundamentalism. Both sets of characteristics – regional and local – have direct bearings on the way business is done in each country.

However, before delving into the characteristics of the Middle East as a marketplace, it is worth describing what it takes for a company to do business successfully in this part of the world. This is quite a different matter from what a company does to meet inherent market conditions – it has more to do with attitudes, which must be adjusted before a company goes to the Middle East. They are important, and must be right from the start.

Any foreign business wishing to succeed in this marketplace must be able to back its effort with total commitment. The dusty streets of Jeddah and Baghdad aren't paved with gold, not even black gold. Half-hearted, poorly financed attempts are doomed to

16

failure and should not be undertaken.

Proper preparation is essential. A company wishing to realise its share of the Middle East market must be able to work to a thoroughly researched plan which takes account of cost, competition and local conditions. This is expensive and time consuming. Middle East business is never done on the questionable basis of two-week trips to five countries or meeting engaging Arabs in London, Paris and New York bars.

So an expensive commitment to enter the region is a necessary first step, followed by appropriate planning. The enterprise is useless without a corporate decision against considering the Middle East as a sideshow or an easy market; it should be viewed as a region with its own personality and complex needs; the successful companies are the ones which understand and meet both. And it must be appreciated that serious differences exist within the overall market (as in South America); national identities within the bigger Arab one.

A company must analyse the countries of the Middle East in terms of their potential for its products or services. Relatively poor Egypt, Syria and the Yemen may be good markets for consumer goods because of their large populations, but there are only so many cigarettes the 200,000 inhabitants of wealthy Qatar can smoke. On the other hand, Qatar is probably a better market for Rolls-Royces and very expensive gold watches. But Qatar was a tremendous disappointment to the French pots-and-pans salesman who envisaged a marketplace twenty-five times its real size. The UAE imports sixteen wrist-watches for every citizen; Egypt, a fraction of one.

Since the Middle East continues to attach a disproportionate importance to people and less to organisations, their products and expertise, an early decision on the company's Middle East representative is vital. Not only is dealing with the Middle East demanding on the representative's flexibility and sensibility but, very often, the volume of business requires the appointment of a senior, sophisticated salesman, regardless of corporate title. An ignorant, rough-and-tumble salesman can be a disaster. (An English cigarette salesman asked what people smoked in the bars of Islamicly-dry Saudi Arabia.) I think the Middle East can very well do without the types who call Mohammeds Mo and Abdullahs

Abdul, who slurp their Turkish coffee in a vulgar, misguided attempt to please their hosts by demonstrating their knowledge of how things are done, and call Saudi Airlines *Insha Allah* (God willing) Airlines in front of their Saudi friends.

Problems can also occur when representatives who have endeared themselves to their Arab agents are recalled. Their heirs seldom take over successfully. The personal contact factor is so important that Arab agents have been known to sever relations with companies when their trusted contact is removed. As far as Arabs are concerned, their relationship depends on the man, and changing him changes everything. Therefore, a company would do well to appoint a man who views his Middle East assignment as a permanent one; ideally, an Arab national.

In addition to these requirements, a sense of reason must prevail in assessing one's ability to fight international competitors. I know British and American TV-set manufacturers who, unable to beat the Japanese in the UK or the USA, believe they can beat them in the Middle East. This is stupid, bad business and companies such as these are better off leaving the Middle East alone. There are also the companies in the do-it-yourself market, which is at least fifty Arab years away, who insist on travelling to the Middle East and explaining in the fullest detail to everyone they meet the advantage of the head of the household undertaking so much of the domestic work. This is unthinkable – goes completely against the Arab cultural grain – and again such companies should stay away.

A foreign corporation must also be realistic in judging its importance to the would-be agent/distributor/promoter, who is likely to be part of a trading company. Middle Eastern trading companies are spiritual kin to the old Hudson's Bay Company or East India Trading Company – they sell chicken wings one day and promote the building of railroads the next. Not only must a Western company select someone who isn't preoccupied with other, potentially more profitable, companies; it must find a local agent with some apparent capability for its type of business. Every second company in the Middle East calls itself Trading and Construction Establishment, but this doesn't mean they trade and/or construct. Few of them even deserve the name establishment. Most are one-man operations that function when the man is there, close when he takes a nap and die when he does.

Properly motivated and funded, with the right research and personnel, a company still has to contend with a variety of regional and local business practices. These, too, demand considerable care.

Asked by a reporter to define what an Arab is, the late President Gamal Abdel Nasser paused and said, 'Anyone who thinks he is one.' This definition falls short of my mark. To me, an Arab is anyone who thinks *like* one. There is a particular way of thinking that is common to all of them even when, like Lebanese Christians for example, they reject the Arab label.

We are concerned here with Arab thinking and attitudes affecting the conduct of business, the ones confronting the outside corporation. These are attitudes misrepresented to and by the outside world.

An appreciation of Arab/Moslem behaviour is essential. An outsider must remember the obvious, like the Arab's Thursday/Friday weekend, and the subtle, such as not walking in front of a person praying – even when the act of devotion is conducted in no less public a place than Jeddah airport. Care at all times is a virtue. Conversations about women, alcohol, dogs and shoes should be avoided unless approval is given by the other side. Women and booze are private, the dog is profane and shoes simply imply disrespect. A Saudi friend once invited an American banker to dinner at home and introduced him to his wife. The following day in an attempt at common politeness the banker told his host that his wife was lovely. He was shocked when the Arab replied, 'My wife is not a subject for conversation,' and threatened to 'make him ugly'.

The list of 'forbiddens' is long and it is not the purpose of this book to go through it in detail. The thing to remember is to maintain a respectful distance at all times – never to mistake Arab hospitality and friendliness for familiarity. I remember my father complaining bitterly about the late President Johnson, who passed through Beirut when still Vice-President. At one point Johnson put his arm around my father while questioning him on a point of local politics. My father, eight inches shorter than Johnson, thought being a 'hand person' the height of vulgarity.

Then there is the Arab's strange sense of time, or lack of it. Arabs do not adhere to exact schedules though they do believe in the meaning of time. Never mind the time of an appointment; the important thing to them is that a meeting should take place. They will double-book because they are too hospitable to say no, and will show genuine concern if one of the parties chooses to opt out of a meeting as a result. So meetings take place at odd hours; too early in the morning, too late at night.

Unless a company and its representatives attune themselves to 'Middle East time' they are likely to face great difficulties in doing business with Arabs. I was at a meeting in Al Khobar, Saudi Arabia, when an American visitor, feeling that his time was being wasted by his host's polite but unbusinesslike conversation, complained that he hadn't come all the way from New York to talk about his health and his family. The host rose to the insult and said, 'If you are not the type of man who is concerned about his health and his family then you are not the type of man with whom we wish to do business.'

The business organisation which exists in the Middle East has certain general characteristics and is at about the same stage of development throughout the territory. As is the case with the Middle Eastern State, the Middle Eastern organisation is mostly the man, occasionally the men, running it. Arabs traditionally do not believe in an organisational structure bigger than its top man.

Intra Bank *was* Yusef Beidas, people know Adnan Khashoggi but do not know his company, Triad Holdings, and most companies carry the name of their founders, both out of pride and because the founders are alive and well and make all the decisions. Anyone wishing to know what a company is all about must know its proprietor and his likes and dislikes. Direct contact with the boss makes life easier and saves time and effort.

Public companies exist, though new. They are few, represent a small percentage of business transacted, and are still dependent upon the reputation of the head man, regardless of whether the company is owned by stockholders or created by a government decision to enter a certain field. Achievement or failure is attributed to the top man, not to staff, business conditions or circumstances beyond his control. Acts of Allah are exempt.

Having understood the structure and decision-making process of a Middle Eastern company, one must also take into account its relationship to the State. Laws governing this relationship are changing constantly in an attempt to keep pace with the changing times. This means a steady enactment of new laws and amendment of the old. This is the overt relationship of the company to the State. In addition, there are those companies who have a covert one, whereby the welfare of the company is totally dependent upon its relationship to the people in power. This seriously affects its ability to win or lose contracts. The son of Osman Ahmad Osman, a leading Egyptian contractor, is married to the late President Sadat's daughter. The company was riding high when Sadat was alive and has suffered considerably since.

At this time there are no laws governing monopolistic practices, which usually manifest themselves through a family secretly controlling most or all companies operating in a certain field. Certainly Osman Ahmad Osman and his interests wielded monopolistic powers in the construction business in Egypt. He handled a very high percentage of all major construction business in that country. The Ghoseibi family controls all shipping and bunkering on the Gulf side of Saudi Arabia, with the blessing of King Fahd. Tihama Advertising and Marketing represents 80% of all advertising in Saudi because its chairman is the King's son Saud.

Often the businessman has to interpret the law on the spot. Some Saudi newspapers accept pictures of ladies in advertising, while others refuse them – not out of adherence, or lack of it, to religious tenets but because each paper reads the law governing this activity differently. Against this vague background an advertiser is ill-advised to take a chance.

In summary, an outside businessman's understanding has to extend beyond the heroic individualism which governs the running of Middle Eastern corporations, to the changing rules with which they live. This has considerable bearing on his conduct of business. For example, only a naive Western corporation would rely on local audits to determine the value of business conducted by an associate. Regulations of audits are not strict and leave room for manipulating figures. Most countries have no agency regulating accounting standards, some have no taxation department and when one exists it hasn't the tools or power to enforce the law. Try auditing the mental books of someone who commits nothing to paper and keeps it all in his head. Better yet, try auditing the books of a Saudi prince.

21

As I have said, rules and regulations differ from country to country. An understanding of Arab ways, the nature of the Middle Eastern corporation and its relationship to the State helps considerably, but these are generalities; the countries of the Middle East should be seen as individual entities.

While this is not a textbook in which to analyse each country's peculiarities in detail, I will try to deal with the overriding elements common to big business situations in each country. Saudi Arabia, Egypt and Iraq deserve an in-depth look. Saudi Arabia has the most money, Egypt has people and geographic position, and Iraq money and people. And these are the countries which set the political and commercial trends throughout the area – the leaders.

SAUDI ARABIA

One third the size of the United States, Saudi Arabia occupies most of the Arabian Peninsula. It is the land of modern legend about oil wealth and its use and abuse.

This vast expanse is, except for oilfields and the south western hilly region bordering Yemen and facing Africa, a ghastly blank of sunbaked, unfriendly land. Prior to oil the country's only source of income was the levy on the pilgrims who trek from all over the globe to visit the Moslem holy cities of Mecca and Al Madina. Now, the pilgrimage is a money-losing proposition, with the housing and transport of hundreds of thousands of faithful subsidised by the oil revenue of the Saudi Government.

Saudi Arabia is run by the house of Saud, who came to power in stages during the First World War. The house of Saud are Wahabis, a small Moslem sect of puritanical inclinations. The founder of the house, Abdul Aziz Al Saud, married an unknown number of times and produced an unknown number of children. Most of his sons have done the same and one day computer technology will be advanced enough to cope with the family tree. Rough estimates place the number of princes at over five thousand.

You must have an understanding of Saudi Arab geography and

regional backgrounds, religious habits and the workings of the house of Saud to do business there.

Very few Saudi companies operate equally effectively in the three main regions of the country: Western, Central and Eastern. The people in each region came from different tribes and the government's concern is to keep the tribes happy. Even central government business is divided on a regional/tribal basis. The Zahids are good in the Western region but have no influence in the others. The Ananis are central region people and if you want to do business in the east, the Al Ghoseibis are your best bet.

As the division is true regardless of discipline, companies would do well to observe these prejudices and, whenever feasible, appoint several agents instead of one. This, naturally, is not applicable when you are selling a product related to the nation state: jet 'planes to Saudi Airlines, films to Saudi TV, etc.

In dealing with outsiders the Saudis are becoming chauvinistic. This is a natural result of oil wealth, which gives them a sense of separateness. This chauvinism shows in their behaviour towards expatriate labour as well as their resentment of old mercantile families with relatively recent Saudi roots, such as Turkeman Adnan Al Khashoggi of Lockheed fame, leading contractor Ali Reza who is originally Iranian, and Gaith Pharoan whose Research and Development Corporation (REDEC) empire includes the biggest insurance business and a fleet of oil tankers, and who is Syrian in origin.

Influential as some of the old mercantile families are, many avenues have been closed to them because they are 'imports'. Their power has been reduced. A close look at the origins of a representative/agent/promoter and his relationship to the region and central government is necessary. This is 50% of the equation for selecting a good one.

There are even newer Saudis than the old mercantile families who have done exceptionally well. They are Palestinians (Oujeh, Abu Khadra, etc.), Egyptian (Ashmawi, Buchari, etc.) and occasionally Syrian or Lebanese. While their achievements are admirable and they undoubtedly have special talents, I am not at all certain that a political crisis couldn't lead to their ejection from the country.

The Saudi is more Moslem than most Arabs. After all, Mecca

23

and Al Madina transcend Rome, they are the recognised centre for all sects of Islam and making the pilgrimage is one of the tenets of Islamic religion.

Despite my unmistakable Arabism, I myself almost got into trouble for alleged disrespectful behaviour. I was at the lavish Intercontinental Hotel in Riyadh, the capital of Saudi Arabia. Having run out of calling cards I went to the hotel front desk to write my London address for a Saudi visitor. While doing this I noticed the desk clerk staring at me and getting redder and redder in the face. He was angry; I was doing something wrong, but I didn't know what. When I enquired, the clerk controlled his anger and told me haltingly that I had turned the hotel paper upside down and that 'In the name of Allah the benevolent and merciful' was at the bottom (this is affixed to all official stationery). I had to apologise hurriedly before the man reported me to the police.

The Saudi attitude to women is also governed by religion. My friend, whose compliment on the banker's wife was mistaken for unwelcome familiarity, has never recovered. I recently invited him to dinner to meet an attractive Palestinian girl but he declined, mumbling about 'a PLO knife in my back'.

Most Saudi businessmen have no respect for money. They are hedonistic by nature, and often the money came easy. Many of them squander the millions they earn and retire to their village or tribe with little damage to their social position or self-esteem. Not only are today's millionaires tomorrow's paupers but the opposite is true. One contract can yield millions. You often hear, 'He is spending the airfield job money,' or 'He just made it, he got the hospital supply job.'

Outsiders should remember this lack of respect for money, particularly when pursuing government contracts, as it helps avoid following their Saudi associates' inclination to chase major contracts by spending lots of cash. A Saudi businessman complained bitterly when British GEC refused to follow him in spending £40,000 preparing a tender offer for an electric utility. 'If I can afford it, surely GEC can,' he said. 'Well,' responded the GEC executive, 'you can do what you want with your money. You don't have a board of directors or shareholders to live with.'

The Saudis are notoriously bad at business communications. This very often leads to a loss of business; for example, they may fail to advise a company of the closing date for a tender offer, or neglect to answer pertinent questions about a deal, because it's too much bother. This is an extension of their lack of respect for time and they often take days if not weeks to answer an urgent telex.

There is no way under Allah's sun to make Saudis good communicators, but one can try to make them better. I would advise that the value of communications be emphasised from the start of a relationship and that any business agreement should contain some guarantee covering this area. By continuously hammering on this theme, outsiders might manage to improve the performance of their Saudi associates.

Lastly, there are thousands upon thousands of sheikhs on top of the five thousand or so princes and the numbers of both are increasing. Dealing with a sheikh or prince is hardly the key to success; after all, they mostly compete against each other. You must learn which are the effective ones in the business arena.

Certain princes may have a more difficult time gaining an audience with King Fahd than would a commoner. They may very well be in disgrace because of drinking, gambling or general bad behaviour. Others are distant relations who exercise little or no influence; yet others are name salesmen who have no inclination to do actual work for a company. There are numerous companies who have signed up with a prince only to find out they need someone else to help. They have to pay both.

If princes present a problem, even worse difficulties arise when outsiders assume that someone with the title of sheikh must be influential. Sheikh is not a fixed title; anyone can call himself that and get away with it.

No picture of Saudi Arabia is complete without a comment on the monarch. This is the world's most absolute feudal kingdom. It is benevolent and the poor get help; harsh and the hands of thieves are amputated; backward because 50% of the people are illiterate; and modern because every (male) Saudi can get a massive government grant to attend a university if he is able. It has an elaborate Islamic judiciary but the will of the King is absolute.

King Fahd presides over all of this. He is assisted by princes, sheikhs, notables from West, Centre and East Saudi. He accommodates change, protects Islamic tradition, dresses in Arab robes, speaks impeccable English, is pro-American, anti-Russian, wealthy beyond imagination. In a way he represents his country.

EGYPT

Egypt has less in common with other Arab nations than any other country covered by this book. It has a base of small industry and cheap labour. It is the least affected by oil wealth, and therefore very poor.

True, Egypt is a minor oil exporter but not on a scale to generate wealth. The rest of Egypt's money comes from cotton, Suez Canal revenues, tourism and the remittances of workers in oil-producing countries. It is therefore an indirect beneficiary of oil wealth. On top of that, Egypt's unique position of being Moslem, Arab, African and geographically strategic earns aid money from the US and Europe.

As an importer of hard consumer goods, Egypt is a secondary market. The Egyptians try to make everything themselves. They assemble Fiat automobiles, air conditioners and refrigerators, radios and TV sets. Proctor & Gamble, Lever Brothers, Johnson Wax and other consumer product-makers license their products for manufacture. The small minority which prefers Mercedes cars and foreign-made consumer goods pays dearly for them because of the extremely high import duty. Food, the country's leading import, comes mostly from the U.S. and is either in the form of aid or paid for by Egypt's soft currency.

An important thing to remember about Egypt is where foreign aid money actually goes. US aid money is earmarked to buy US products or utilise the services of US companies. Since the US aid package is the largest, the US companies are very well placed to do business in Egypt. But other countries give aid too, and the money goes to the companies of the donor country.

When Egyptians are using their own money and the national identity of a company is not a factor, then a company should prepare itself for extremely complex competition. Most business opportunities are three- or four-cornered: the Egyptians will use as much Egyptian input as possible; they tend to divide a project in many parts, and of course there is the ever-present Egyptian bureaucracy.

To untangle such situations, an outside corporation must have a good agent/representative. Only a few Eygptians can unravel all the complexities surrounding a business deal in their country. Egypt is the only Arab country where Arabs from elsewhere do not operate. They can't.

Aside from needing a good agent, outside companies should resign themselves to the most inefficient governmental system in the Middle East, and day-to-day corruption which is almost universal.

The Egyptian bureaucrat shows no initiative whatsoever – there is no sparkle here. He is lazy and ineffectual. He will accept a bribe and most of the time will do nothing in return. Often he will accept a bribe from more than one source to do the same thing. The corruption of Egyptian officialdom exists at all levels. Bribing someone in Egypt is easy – just give them money, no matter how little. There is no pride to stand in the way.

Influence-peddling in Egypt is vested in a minority of old-established families: Othmans, Fayads, Shahines, etc. One per cent of the population of 45,000,000 is very rich; the rest are extremely poor. These 'business families' existed under King Farouk, and President Nasser and continue to exert influence under the present regime. In order to win deals they buy cabinet members to use political pressure, a deputy minister for day-to-day intelligence about a deal, and lowly officials to keep them apprised of who is aiding competitors.

Compounding the bleak Egyptian situation is one of the world's most inefficient communications systems. It is literally collapsing under its own weight. It takes days to telex outside the country, internal telephones are out of order most of the time and often there is no way to communicate with someone a mile or two away. Because of traffic jams, an urgent message may take days to deliver.

In summary, there is no money in Egypt for huge investment projects. The country's agro-industrial potential has been realised. The importation of finished goods is limited. Bureaucracy is crippling. The only possibilities are the occasional building of small industrial plant, pursuing the occasional foreign aid development project and bartering for oil, cotton or cheap labour. Egypt is a difficult place with limited potential.

IRAQ

How sad it is that Iraq's modern fame rests on being one of the belligerents in the bloody Gulf War. For this land between the two rivers not only produced the first written word, the hanging gardens of Babylon, and romantic Baghdad of a thousand and one nights, it is also essentially the most promising country in the whole Middle East.

Iraq has oil wealth which equals and perhaps surpasses that of Saudi Arabia. The Tigris and Euphrates rivers endow it with immense agro-industrial potential and it has vast iron ore and phosphate deposits. Couple all of that with an educated middle class making for the best infrastructure in the Middle East and you have a winning combination. I suspect that once the evil war is over the Iraqis will revert to their long-term planning and the country will once again become the envy of the Middle East and the world.

Until recently, Iraq's government followed a strictly socialist line and there was no private sector in business. The reins have now been eased and a good number of companies are owned half by the government, half by private investors. In addition, a substantial private sector has blossomed to compete with and spur on the public one.

Private sector and mixed-ownership business now accounts for 50% of all business in Iraq though the size of individual invest-ment remains relatively small. The emergence of private business during the past five years has had a remarkably healthy effect on the public sector. It has meant better products and services.

No investment in the private sector is possible for non-Iraqis. But as technology and expertise is needed, non-Iraqi companies could do well to seek opportunities in this area through helping Iraqi industrialists develop small industries. This blow for free enterprise is made more attractive by the fact that the Iraqis are the area's best industrialists, and assisting them would definitely assert the advantages of heroic capitalism.

Besides, Iraqi technocrats are the best in the Middle East. The old Iraqi Petroleum Company discovered oil there in 1908 and began educating the total population. Also, the landed gentry (which didn't exist in peninsula countries) traditionally sent their children to the best British public schools and to Oxford and Cambridge. More recently, thousands upon thousands of Iraqi students have been educated en masse in British, US and German universities through generous government grants, which had the singular stipulation of requiring the beneficiary to return to Iraq to work. Iraq is the only Middle East country to have run its oil business without outside help for over twenty years.

The presence of capable technocrats is noticeable to outside businessmen and represents a welcome change from other places. Another distinguishing Iraqi business characteristic is the presence of laws 8 and 52 forbidding intermediary activity and making certain aspects of it punishable by death. This doesn't mean there are no agents; there are. They are officially registered with the government, which limits their scope of operation and level of commissions.

At this moment there are about seventy legal agents allowed to represent foreign companies, who would be well-advised to work with them. The fact that there are so few is a positive advantage when one considers that there are some thirteen to fifteen thousand agents to choose from in Saudi Arabia.

There are people who operate outside laws 8 and 52. Their illegal activities are recorded in full in other parts of this book. Given the government attitude and the punishment attached to it, I would always counsel against following this route.

Iraq's preoccupations differ from Saudi Arabia's and those of the Gulf states. The government wants to develop local industry in a serious way, be it making bricks and storm windows or producing films good enough to enter the Cannes Film Festival. The country's bureaucrats speak of 'transfer of technology', 'technological gap' and 'borrowing expertise'. A company manufacturing easy-to-make products would do well to help the Iraqis make them. The days in trading in such items are over.

Doing business of any kind in Iraq requires effort. A company needs to register with the Central Bank to get paid, with the Registrar of Companies to operate, and probably with state trading companies to effect business. This takes time.

The Iraqis are creatures of habit. The most difficult piece of business in Iraq is the first one. After that things become easier and the likelihood of more orders is real. Therefore, I recommend a break-even approach to doing business there in the first instance. Builder Taylor Woodrow and school equipment suppliers PEL, both of the UK, followed this method and have lived to tell a happy tale of what followed.

In personal terms, today's Iraqi is an odd creature. He is not pure Arab. There are pronounced Turkish, Kurdish and Iranian influences in Iraq and the Iraqis' everyday Arabic reflects it. They are humourless people, gruff in manner, irreverent and proud. Their attitude towards religion is for the most part moderate; women are assuming a role in society – Iraq had a female member of the cabinet in 1958 – and scotch whisky is practically a national drink.

Iraqis consider themselves superior to the Gulf Arabs. They are educated and technically competent while the others aren't. Their small industries are well run, beyond comparison. The level of petty corruption in Iraq is considerably lower than in other places. In contrast to the Gulf states, Iraq has a modern army, a tried fighting force, which means it can operate large organised bodies of people.

The possibilities in Iraq are immense and diverse. I cannot imagine anyone interested in the Middle East who could afford to ignore them. The future is definitely in Iraq.

KUWAIT

In its own way, Kuwait is a sophisticated market. The country is in an advanced state of development: they have had the big oil money longest – since the fifties. Most of the infrastructural building programmes have been carried out.

Two other elements are fundamental to understanding Kuwait: the successful welfare-state approach adopted by the ruling Al Sabah families and the commercial agility of the country's leading trading families Al Ghanim, Al Marzough, Al Wazan, Al Mulla, etc.

So we have a well-developed country where no one is hungry and where the trading families have learned the ropes of international commerce. The ruling family, attractively unobtrusive, can rightly be described as conscientious and benevolent.

This small country of about 1,000,000 people, just half of whom are foreigners and all concentrated in Kuwait city, has shown a consistent balance of payment surplus for over thirty years. In 1982 the country's income from investment abroad is said to have been 90% of its oil income.

The foreigners in Kuwait work for the Kuwaitis. They are Palestinian teachers, lawyers and administrators, Lebanese who assist Kuwaiti merchants, and Iranians and Indians who perform menial tasks. Kuwaitis have been generous to their guests but become totally intolerant at the slightest reflection on how they run their country.

Kuwait has a parliament which is relatively free. The Kuwaiti press is outspokenly sophisticated. There is an overall easy atmosphere and open debate. With parliamentary and journalistic watchdogs capable of screaming murder, the commercial atrocities possible elsewhere cannot happen here.

Because of the level of sophistication, the developed market and the presence of parliament and press, business is more openly competitive and cleaner than in most places. There have been no major bribery scandals in Kuwait. Defence procurement is almost above manipulation and held in super secrecy.

Though this is not a country for easy money, Kuwaiti business can still be good. After all, the Kuwaitis have an exceptionally high level of income which leads to conspicuous consumption: they change their furniture at least once every two years, they sport gold and diamond-studded watches, buy shoes by the dozen and ties by the twenties. Even capital goods plants tend to be expensive and are maintained expensively.

Kuwait is a good place to do business. A company has to be willing to compete, have the right product and manage to convince a good Kuwaiti commercial house to represent it.

THE UAE, QATAR AND BAHRAIN

The United Arab Emirates do not constitute a country. They are a shaky alliance of convenience, until recently a collection of barren stretches of land elevated to sudden prominence by the discovery of black gold. Each of the seven parts of this unnatural creation moves in two directions: as an independent unit and as part of the UAE.

With a total population of about 500,000 people, these sheikh-doms are forced to cede to the UAE (the federal entity) in matters of foreign policy and defence. In all other areas each sheikhdom manages its own business.

The dichotomy increases business opportunity because it means the UAE is several countries with duplicated needs. Each country (even with a population of 40,000) needs its police force, civil servants, ADCs to the sheikh, and each wants its international airport, big enough to accommodate jumbo jets. There is waste here which can be exploited by outside companies.

On top of this, the money is new and there is no judicious approach to distributing it as in Kuwait. Nor is there the equivalent of the ultra-successful Kuwaiti Investment Fund to channel surplus money into the international markets. What we have here are a collection of rulers amenable to the advice of their foreign counsellors, who always advise spending.

The UAE is the most open market in the Middle East. The need for expatriates (there are more of them than natives) is the greatest in the area. The number of intermediaries is also high because of the number of rulers. The presence of intermediaries and their degree of success is made possible by the simplicity of the rulers and the fact that they do well out of their sidekicks.

Strange opportunities exist in the UAE. A sheikh can spend untold millions on a one-acre garden. A supplier of furniture to some of their palaces told me 'The uglier it is, the better it sells.' Other sheikhs have their own elaborate mobile communications systems to carry around when they go falcon hunting. One sheikha (female sheikh) bought four hundred dresses in London to take back as presents.

This is a dizzy-with-wealth Bedouin society where anything goes.

32

*   *   *

Qatar, the small peninsula which juts into the Arabian Gulf like an appendage to the larger Arabian Pensinsula, is a quiet place. This country has a population of about 300,000 gentle people who appear unspoiled by wealth.

Business in Qatar belongs to a handful of families: the ruling Abu Thani family, the Mannaes, the Mannis and few others. With a government more conservative and less segmented than the UAE, the Quataris have their own system of distributing wealth through the allocation of projects. Essentially, the system works against any one party getting too much and favours 'sharing' the projects available.

As a result, there is very little friction and competition is healthy, with a marked absence of ugly behaviour. Also the cohesiveness of the country makes for a sensible development programme.

Unlike the Emirates, the Qataris are not smugglers nor do they wish their country to become a shopping centre. Because of this, the Qatari consumer market is a very small one indeed. Many makers of consumer products ignore this market altogether.

Even major development projects are few. This means that construction companies, builders of petrochemical plant and heavy capital goods suppliers find little justification for establishing their own offices or creating any permanent presence in Qatar. This in turn leads to greater dependence on local representatives or sponsors and greater demand on their ability. This healthy state of affairs means that the involvement of the Qataris is high.

For very simple reasons, the level of commission paid to intermediaries in Qatar is low. Contenders in this field are few, the place is small and knowledge of what the others are doing produces downward pressure on commissions.

In total, Qatar has a limited consumer market, an intermediary group which is small and not greedy, and a conservative government which uses the old family establishments as a distribution system. On top of all that, the Qataris are a polite, unspoiled lot. If a corporation has a product Qatar needs then it should locate a leading name and give him the business, thereby realising what little opportunity the country affords.

*   *   *

Bahrain is a tiny, attractive island with a history. The UAE is a Bedouin settlement and Qatar is another, made pleasant by a sense of closeness and family. Bahrain is also Bedouin, with the difference that it was a centre of learning with its own university during the days of the Abbasseyed Empire, about a thousand years ago.

Bahrain is unique in the Gulf, because of its history and the fact that it never had much money. There is little oil here and Bahrain is a very small exporter of it. Whatever oil Bahrain has was discovered about seventy years ago and its effects have been totally absorbed.

Again, we have a country of just over 200,000 natives and an equal number of expatriates. The expatriates tend to be segmented, comprising Brits, Iranians, Indians and Pakistanis, Palestinians, Lebanese and Egyptians. Like their hosts, they have a little more polish, belonging to the professional rather than labouring class. Forty-three international banks have branches in Bahrain and a lot of service companies operate there on a regional basis.

The ruling Al Khalifa family go back four hundred years and they cast a gentle shadow making them genuinely popular. There are old trading families like the Zayanis, Khanoos and Fakhroos and they do good business; neither they nor members of the ruling family are involved in anything resembling abuse.

Major projects are very few indeed and big Saudi-size money is absent. Bahrain offers a pleasant, relatively free atmosphere with limited monetary rewards.

OMAN

Oman is a huge land, twice as large as the UK. It is a beautiful country with a considerable history and, because it is separated from the rest of the Arabian peninsula by the Empty Quarter, it relates to the Indian sub-continent across the Arabian Sea.

Oman is run by Sultan Qaboos and his friends, a collection of former British army officers who, like him, attended the Royal Military College at Sandhurst. The place is full of captains, majors and colonels, an unattractive collection of men full of pretension and antiquated officers' club manners. As long as Qaboos lives, the British Empire is here to stay!

Like Egypt, Oman has some oil and is a nett exporter. Like Egypt, this country gets a considerable amount of outside aid money because of its strategic position astride the Arabian Gulf and the oilfields surrounding it. Thirdly, like Egypt, Oman is solidly pro-West and supported Egypt's Camp David initiative. Its pro-West stance is partly due to the threat posed by its pro-Russian neighbour, South Yemen. Unlike Egypt, Oman's population is small, a little over 1,000,000 people, hence their dependence on the British to officer their army.

Qaboos has had more than his share of trouble; there have been a number of rebellions aimed at overthrowing him. His government is unpopular. People resent his aloofness, disapprove of his advisors and grumble about his corrupt ways. He depends on the army to stay in power. As a result, Oman's army gets a bigger slice of the national cake than it deserves. Eighty-thousand strong, its scope of operation extends beyond the traditional role and is involved in what is described as 'strategic development': highway, airport and harbour building among others.

The second most influential man in Oman is Sultan Qaboos's uncle, Sayed Fahr bin Taymour, who is Deputy Prime Minister, Minister of Defence and Crown Prince. A company interested in arms deals and development schemes in Oman's public sector must go to Sultan Qaboos or his uncle. This can be done by working with one of the companies directly controlled by them or working with a trading family which can reach them (Al Futtaims, Al Mousas, etc.).

The combination of oil money, aid money and a sizeable army is a good background for intermediary business. The size of the country, its strategic position and its large population all help. Oman is fertile intermediary ground. In terms of both development projects and consumer market, this place cannot be ignored.

THE YEMENS

North Yemen is supposedly the location for the biblical Garden of

35

Eden. Occupying the south western corner of the Arabian Peninsula, it is a beautiful country with high mountains, the world's earliest skyscrapers and a population of 6,000,000 people. It is a republic, with a turbulent history. At present it is stable. However, stable or not, the same old trading families do most of the business (Thabets, Shagas, etc.).

North Yemen's money comes from two sources: 750,000 labourers working in Saudi Arabia and other oil-rich countries and foreign aid from the US, Saudi Arabia and some European countries. This has created a promising situation with a growing consumer market (workers' remittances) and development projects (aid money). In addition, North Yemen is at the beginning of a tourist boom. Young Swedes and Germans with knapsacks are already there. In the tourist business they represent the vanguard.

The Yemenis are seafarers, subsequently traders. A select number of trading families controls everything. They are chameleons, managing to live no matter what type of government is in power. Corruption is rife and it is who you are and who you know that matters. Intermediary influence is present in the armament business, in winning major development projects, and in supplying grain to the government.

North Yemen is backward, a virgin territory, and it could well be a receptive market for both consumer and capital goods products. South Yemen, Aden in colonial days, is rather different. It is mostly desert and therefore not as attractive and full of history as the northern region. It is poor and solidly pro-Russian socialist.

There is nothing to sell to South Yemen except arms and they come from Russia on easy credit terms. Neither is there money to import Western-made consumer goods. Russia has been looking for a way to help this wretched country but can't find one.

South Yemen is desperate to unite with North Yemen and the latter is receptive to the idea. However, they disagree on the type of government which should emerge if such a move is undertaken. There are 2,000,000 people in South Yemen living under a repressive regime which adds to their misery. South Yemen is the Albania of the Middle East.

JORDAN

Comparing Jordan to the rest of the Middle East is like comparing King Hussein to the rest of the Arab leaders. He is more advanced and so is Jordan.

King Hussein is relatively young, athletic, urbane and more attuned to the twentieth century than other Arab leaders. He is King of a country where two-thirds of the population is Palestinian and he has learned to live with their inherent unhappiness. Hussein tries to please, taking pains to accommodate tribal chiefs with a limited seventeenth-century outlook and socialist academics educated in the best universities of Europe and the United States.

Hussein's back-up is his brother Hassan, the Crown Prince. Hassan is aggressive, tends to be anti-Palestinian and hence is unpopular with at least two-thirds of the population. He lacks the appeal and experience of Hussein.

Jordan, with a population of 4,000,000, has a variety of trades and professions with its growing small industry, its teachers, doctors and lawyers, its modern citrus farms and phosphate mining. The country's number one asset is the human talent of 300,000 professionals working in oil-rich countries and remitting most of their earnings. Its small industry satisfies its needs, and exports to other Arab countries. Jordanian oranges and apples are found throughout the Middle East and phosphate is exported worldwide.

The Jordanians do with everything what they have done with their army. It may not be the best-equipped army in the world but it uses whatever equipment it has with admirable competence.

Public sector spending is limited. Money isn't available, nor are investment opportunities. The obvious development areas (phosphate and agriculture) have been realised. This leaves the slow-developing areas of electrification, health and bringing telephones to villages. Naturally, a standing army, 100,000 strong, creates demands.

The private sector here is a better place for business than the public sector. Jordan is middle class, its people enjoy middle-class comforts and spend money on cars, airconditioning, perfumes, etc. There are many reputable, well-run trading companies (Nazzal, Muasher) with whom one can deal to obtain a share in this stable, though small market.

An opportunity unique to Jordan is in small industry. The central geographic position of the country plus the availability of human talent makes it a natural locale for such industries. Add to that the many incentives offered by the government to outside and local investors, and this is indeed an opportunity worth examining. Gypsum board, paint, prefab houses and pharmaceuticals are exported east to Iraq, south to Saudi Arabia, north to Syria and further afield to Kuwait and the rest of the Gulf states.

Jordanian intermediaries are mainly involved in deals with the military. Sadly, friends and relatives of King Hussein have cornered the market. Not only do they represent the suppliers to the Jordan army, but they are adept at selling the army's out-of-date equipment to poor African countries. Things are a bit fairer when it comes to non-military business; on the whole, the best offer will win the contract – though if two offers are equally satisfactory, the company with the closest contacts with government are favoured.

Jordanian intermediaries operate in the arms field in other Arab countries. The top ones are close to Hussein, who certainly whispers words of recommendation to Gulf rulers on behalf of Jordanian arms dealers.

Jordan is a small, healthy place with less under-the-table dealing than other Arab countries. It should be on the agenda for anyone interested in steady Middle East business for its own sake and as a centre for manufacturing for the rest of the Middle East.

SYRIA

Nature is kinder to Syria than its rulers are. A country with a population of 10,000,000, it has immense agro-industrial potential. In addition, it has some oil and the potential for tourism (Damascus, Palmyra, crusaders' castles) is huge.

Syria's rulers, who until recently changed with the frequency of the seasons, mercilessly exploit their country. Nowhere in the Middle East is the relationship between government and trade so close as in Syria. Whoever is in power has always seen fit to be crudely exploitative not only in terms of large contracts but even meddling in small ones which should be beneath their dignity.

So one has to deal with a politician-businessman. Though they have been traders since time immemorial, selling their spices and steel to Europe a thousand years ago, the Syrian mercantile families attach themselves to the ruling class, which most often comes from the army. Their success or failure depends on the strength of this connection.

In structure Syria resembles the military dictatorship of South America. But it goes beyond that. The Syrians believe they are the guardians of all the Arabs and are always making trouble. They could be called the Irish of the Middle East.

The social dynamics of this country preclude the possibility of a change for the better in Syria. It will continue to be ruled by zealously anti-Israeli army types who will exploit the country.

As a marketplace Syria is attractive. It could be considered lower middle class. There is a market for consumer goods and there is considerable room for agro-industrial development and small industries (textiles, building materials, etc.). In addition, electrification, road building, damming and other infrastructural developments have yet to be realised.

Syria's business atmosphere is suffocating. Much can be done here, however, particularly if a company is willing to barter or counter-trade. Funnily enough, the area where big money is made elsewhere in the Middle East is clean here. The reason: Syria gets all its arms from Russia on a state-to-state basis with no need for middlemen. Everything else is subject to the intermediary's interfering finger.

LIBYA

Libya is wealthy, full of potential and promises to continue to be insane as long as Colonel Qaddafi runs it. Opportunity exists on all levels: land reclamation, school and hospital construction, electrification, desalination, telecommunications and maintaining all of that. With a population of 3,000,000 people, it produces very little, and is therefore a natural market for consumer goods.

However, the promise of Libya goes unrealised. This is because of the constant changes in policy which are dictated by the whims

and fancies of Colonel Muamar Al Qaddafi, the country's popul-
ist leader and the sole remaining subscriber to the late Nasser's
Arab unity ideas.

One day when Qaddafi is gone this will become a most attractive
market. Not only is it very close to the European oil users but its oil
is reckoned to be the best. The country's income has fluctuated
between $10,000,000,000 and $30,000,000,000 annually during
the past ten years. Sadly, most of the money goes to political
adventures which do not benefit the average Libyan.

All Libyan trading companies are controlled by the government. Most of the government organisations are run by army
officers or former army officers with little appreciation for what
goes on in the outside world. They can be and often are bribed.
But it is a dangerous business which can earn the Libyan and his
co-conspirators the death sentence.

Qadaffi buys a lot of arms, much more than his army can use. He
wants to be the arsenal of the Arab countries in their battles against
their foes and he arms revolutionary movements all over the map
from Mauritania to the Horn of Africa.

Russia supplies Qaddafi with considerable amounts of armament for which he pays in hard currency. Russian hardware isn't
the whole answer – some electronic equipment and light arms
must come from the West. All arms from the West are bought
under the table to overcome the embargo Western governments
have placed on their sale to Qaddafi.

Qaddafi uses intermediaries to buy arms. He has to pay well
above open market prices and his intermediaries make millions of
dollars. His two main arms buyers are a Palestinian with a PhD
from Columbia University and a former British army major. The
Palestinian advises Qaddafi politically but the major's interest is
limited to money. I am reluctant to say more about the doings of
this violent regime.

Whether a company should pursue Libyan business or not is not
an easy question to answer. The money is there, but the government is unpredictable and can cancel contracts for unjustifiable
reasons. Libya is a dangerous place to work.

In summary, business opportunities in the Middle East remain
good but not easy. As with those who went West in the Rush, not
everyone finds gold. A commitment to do business in the area,

meticulous planning, careful selection and use of personnel and an understanding of the region and its various parts are vital.

3

---**•••**---

The Skimmer

A major stumbling block impeding the completion of many an intermediary-effected deal is the skimmer. As I have said, the skimmer is the powerful person who gets a commission regardless of what company or intermediary gets a contract. Unless he gets what he wants, the skimmer can stop a deal from going through; his pay-off comes from the intermediary.

A deal can be stopped discreetly and cleanly, or messily, depending on the power of the skimmer, and how effectively the intermediary is able to resist his intrusion. But once an intermediary/skimmer feud develops, most deals are too dangerous to finalise and many companies opt out altogether.

Usually a skimmer is either a permanent fixture, recognised as needing to be satisfied from the start of a deal, or he enters the picture at the last minute, having determined that a deal is about to succeed or has a good chance of success.

No skimmer is interested in small deals. They are big money people and that comes from big projects. The occasional exception to this – not a major factor here – is the bureaucrat skimmer, the little man who, due to the accident of serving on a technical committee or the like, has enough influence and courage to delay or impede processing a deal until his little needs are met.

Like everything else about intermediary-related activities, skimming can be institutionalised and often is. The 'institutional' skimmer is most often someone who cannot be avoided when doing business with a particular department or ministry; when no deal can take place without his blessing.

Prince Sultan bin Abdul Aziz, Saudi Arabian Minister of Defence, and number two in line to the throne after Crown Prince Abdullah, is probably the greatest living example of an institutional skimmer. Lockheed's Khashoggi and other household names may be the world's top intermediaries but they still have to pay Prince Sultan a cut on every arms deal they do. Whoever wins a deal has to pay Prince Sultan or it won't go through. Rifaat Al Assad, Syria's Vice-President, brother of President Hafez Al Assad and head of the secret police, is another institutional skimmer.

It should be remembered here that arms dealers and agents have been in the business a long time, are quite well known and socially accepted in places like Saudi Arabia. There is no social stigma attached to the activity. On the contrary, in a society with a warring tradition, dealing in arms confers macho and, because of its natural closeness to government, implies importance. Prince Sultan and Rifaat Al Assad represent no company, yet all of the companies' consultants, agents, distributors and intermediaries pay them a very high percentage of their commission. As skimmers, they are established institutions. Others may very well promote the companies' products but these are the men who can say no. No one dares challenge their authority – no one even tries.

Because their position is unassailable, Prince Sultan and Vice-President Al Assad do not have to stoop to tactical manoeuvring to have intermediaries accommodate them. They simply direct their emissaries to find out how much an intermediary is getting out of a deal. The pay-off business being the dirty business it is, they won't rely on the word of an intermediary as to his commission, but determine what their cut will be from the reports of their own men.

Saudi Arabia is heavily dependent on the USA for most of its armaments, but, because of the various US laws and watchdog agencies inhibiting payment of commission, intermediaries make their big money from arms deals with other countries. Commissions paid by US companies, though generous by normal standards, do not compare with those from elsewhere, and Saudi's intermediaries would rather go for the higher levels of commission. There are no anti-corruption laws in Britain or France, for example.

Skimmers, institutional or otherwise, belong to an exclusive club, and the institutional skimmer is wealthy beyond the dreams of normal mortals. After all, there are very few major ones in the whole of the Middle East. As well as Prince Sultan and Vice-President Al Assad, they include Sultan Qaboos of Oman and his uncle Sayed Fahr, a number of Middle Eastern Ministers of Defence and a few others.

The 'roving' skimmer also makes a great deal of money, but he works hard for it. He does not devote his attention to a specific department or ministry, but wanders around examining the books of all of them. Having determined who is likely to win a contract, the roving skimmer imposes himself on the situation. His close relationship with the government allows him to do this.

The roving skimmer's job is made more complicated by the number of intermediaries he has to intercept. And he has to be in an exceptionally powerful position, otherwise his activity could easily backfire. He must have a direct link to the highest power in the land before attempting to effect this extraordinary activity.

Fatih Hamdar, son-in-law of the former Iraqi President, Ahmed Bakr, was a roving skimmer. This young man was an army colonel, though his rank seems to have owed more to his relationship with the President than to his limited talents. Furthermore, he appears to have been extremely close to the President because the President was utterly devoted to his only daughter, Hamdar's wife.

The Colonel and his snoops determined which contracts were going where, who the companies' intermediaries were, and selected their targets. The Colonel would send his emissaries with a request for a specific amount of money, a percentage of the percentage, to be paid to him in a certain Swiss bank if a contract was awarded. He deviated from normal practice by never approaching the intermediary. Instead he went directly to the company, and the company in turn went to the intermediary and petitioned him to transfer part of the monies (or agreement committed to him) to Hamdar.

The Colonel's relationship with the President ensured a positive response from most companies and eventually the intermediary. Companies succumb to pressure more easily than do seasoned intermediaries. Some companies and intermediaries demanded proof of the skimmer's identity and his ability to queer the deal. After all, attempts at skimming are very often phony and do not stand up to examination. A Palestinian would-be skimmer intruded on a deal, claiming he spoke for Saudi Crown Prince Abdullah. The story reached Abdullah who punished this major official in his entourage by banishing him to London. Abdullah was already involved 'institutionally'.

Our Colonel created problems whenever his roving eye alighted on a promising deal – not least because of his unabashed demand for up to 80% of all available commissions. This left very little for the intermediary and his team, considering the time and effort they would already have invested in a deal.

One intermediary faced with the Colonel's demands refused to be accommodating because he could not afford it. As a result a Mafia-type war developed. The Colonel's men threatened people related to the intermediary with physical harm, and certain of his operations suffered damage. (A mysterious fire consumed an offer to supply grain to the Iraq Army.) These damages could not be mistaken for accidents. The Colonel got his way most of the time. He was an extremely successful and wealthy roving skimmer, for he was in business for about six years in a country which used oil money to plan and execute more major development projects than any other in the Middle East.

It is only fair to report that one of President Sadam Hussein's first acts on assuming the powers of the presidency of Iraq five years ago was to transfer him to a hardship post in northern Iraq, in a minor desk job. He has not been heard of since.

Skimmers don't always win. They have been known to push their luck, and effrontery, too far. Take the case of Garish Mabrouk, doyen of a leading trading family in Saudi Arabia, the son of a former head of the all-powerful council of advisors to the King. An international business figure. Mabrouk should have known better than to attempt to skim on a deal where the 'intermediaries' – though no commission was involved – were King Juan Carlos of Spain and Crown Prince, now King, Fahd. The deal concerned the Spanish state oil petroleum company, Hispanoil, and took place in 1980.

It is well known that the late King Khalid of Saudi Arabia was a retiring figurehead; that Fahd was by then already the source of power in the country. And Fahd liked Spain. He went there for his holidays and was comfortable in its atmosphere. It had warmer weather than most European countries, afforded a greater measure of privacy than Britain, the Unites States or France, and the Spanish Government was more hospitable. Besides, he stayed at his own palace, a $50,000,000 structure outside Marbella.

During his many visits, Crown Prince Fahd appears to have developed a personal friendship with King Juan Carlos. The latter saw to it that the Prince was accorded the highest degree of comfort and protection, from special landing rights for his private jet to arranging for lamb to be butchered according to Islamic rules. He paid him personal visits whenever the opportunity arose.

The Managing Director of Hispanoil, aware of the developing friendship between the two Royals, approached King Juan Carlos through his Prime Minister, Saurez, and asked whether the King would initiate negotiations with Prince Fahd towards the direct purchase of Saudi oil for Spain. Direct purchase meant bypassing the major oil companies and saving Spain no less than $5 to $7 a barrel of oil. Considering that Spain needed 180,000 barrels of oil a day, this meant a minimum saving of $800,000 a day for the Spanish Government.

The King, realising the importance of this deal to the Spanish economy, obliged and broached the subject with Prince Fahd during their next meeting. The discussions took place over a period of six months during two separate visits of Crown Prince Fahd, and a deal was approved. Garish Mabrouk was in attendance on the Prince at three of the meetings with Juan Carlos. In fact, his presence was accidental, but the Spaniards could not know this.

Because of his deep involvement in the major development schemes in Saudi Arabia, Mabrouk arranged to be in Spain when Prince Fahd was there. It was easier for him to talk to the Prince and solicit his favours in Spain than interrupt his busy schedule in Saudi Arabia.

The agreement-in-principle was finalised at the top and the details of the contract between Spain and Saudi Arabia were worked out by their respective companies – Hispanoil and Petromin. It called for what Juan Carlos wanted, oil at the price paid to Saudi Arabia by Exxon, Shell, Mobil, etc. Juan Carlos had good cause to feel pleased at his achievement and so did the Spanish Prime Minister and the Managing Director of Hispanoil. But this apparently clear victory for Spanish diplomacy did not last very long.

A week after the deal was concluded, the Managing Director of Hispanoil was approached by Garish Mabrouk and asked for a commission of $2 a barrel of oil, which would amount to $360,000 a day, close to $120,000,000 a year.

Shocked as he was, the head of Hispanoil reminded his Saudi acquaintance of the history of the agreement between the two governments and the roles of the King and Crown Prince. He appealed to him to withdraw the request. He asserted correctly that as far as Spain was concerned they wished to use no intermediary otherwise they would have gone to major oil companies. Mabrouk would not be dissuaded. He kept telexing, telephoning and travelling to Spain demanding immediate payment of this rather exorbitant commission.

The Spanish faced a real dilemma, due entirely to the lack of understanding and trust between East and West. Juan Carlos and Fahd had shaken hands over a written agreement. But this important Saudi businessman had been present at several of the meetings. Had the Crown Prince sent him to extort commission? Was this just another instance of the way Arabs do business? If Mabrouk were indeed the Prince's spokesman, to bring his intervention to Fahd's notice would be to lose the deal altogether. On the other hand, the commission was ludicrously high.

After three months of hush-hush attempts at dissuasion, the Managing Director of Hispanoil decided to discuss the problem with Prime Minister Suarez. The Prime Minister, equally shocked, took it to the King. The King, his royal dignity affronted, and one of the major achievements at stake, telephoned Prince Fahd with the news of this attempt at skimming.

Prince Fahd was reassuring but, very politely, asked for a report, including copies of the telexes, records of telephone conversations and the various visits to be sent to him in Jeddah immediately. The Spanish Government duly obliged and the Prince had the file in front of him in two days.

Prince Fahd summoned Mabrouk for an audience. He enquired from him about 'rumours' floating around that he was demanding a commission from Hispanoil. When Mabrouk denied the rumours the Prince threw the file at him and asked him to read it. Mabrouk was at a complete loss, and finally took refuge in saying that he wanted the money to donate to the late King Faisal's favourite charity and not for personal gain.

Prince Fahd, fully convinced that an attempt at blackmail had taken place, walked over to Mabrouk, slapped him twice across the face, then spat on him, a traditional gesture of deep insult reserved for the particularly profane. Prince Fahd did not stop there. He ordered Saudi Government agencies not to award any contracts to this man's various companies and to stop them from continuing work on projects already awarded.

Garish Mabrouk has suffered an estimated $65,000,000 of damages. He can no longer operate in the public sector and is limited to much smaller deals in the private sector. He has used the good offices of many an influential person in an attempt to reinstate himself in the court of now King Fahd. The last I heard, all of these attempts had failed and the man continues to suffer incalculably for his attempt at skimming and confusing his position, however powerful, with that of the man who runs Saudi Arabia.

A typical inelegant attempt at skimming which takes place regularly is when a bumbling member of the House of Saudi intervenes at the last minute to secure himself a share of the proceeds of a business deal. This is playing the roving skimmer without sophistication. A businessman who controls a number of Saudi companies was at one time promoting the interests of a major Swedish construction company to win a contract to build a large part of the Jeddah harbour. The company in question is not only big but has particular competence and expertise in this field, as they have built and managed many a harbour throughout the world. If their price was equal, or near equal, to competitors, they stood a very good chance of winning a harbour contract because of their reputation.

The estimated value of their part of the work on the Jeddah harbour was $900,000,000. The Saudi businessman had agreed to promote their offer against that of other companies in return for 2% commission to be paid pro rata as payments were received by them from the Saudi Government in the event that they won the contract. By all standards a 2% commission is rather a modest one, but the size of the contract compensated for this.

Fifteen companies were tendering to build that particular part of the harbour. Soon, a technical committee eliminated ten, leaving five, including the Swedish company, still in the running. After deeper analysis of the offers, the five were reduced to two, the Swedish company and one from South Korea.

The final price being offered by the companies differed, the Korean company's price being lower. But this was a prestige project and the Saudi Government was inclined to award it to a recognised international company with an impeccable reputation. In terms of quality, the Swedes had the edge.

While the competition was in its last stages, the Saudi Government appointed a new Governor of the City of Jeddah; as usual, a member of the Saudi Royal Family. Unlike his predecessor, this man did not know the Saudi businessman sponsoring the Swedish company, and arrived on the scene too late to be party to any intermediary team formation.

Soon enough the Prince/Governor found out about the deal and summoned the businessman to his posh palace for an audience. They sat cross-legged on heavily padded couches exchanging comments of mutual esteem over cups of coffee full of cardomom seed. Politely the Prince asked that he be included in the benefits from the new harbour project. The Saudi businessman agreed. He did not know that the Governor wanted a total of 2% for himself. In other words, all of the commission.

When told of his polite host's 'requirement' the businessman argued that 2% was all that he was getting. Besides, he was already $500,000 out of pocket from promoting the deal, not to mention the time and effort he and his staff had invested in the project. Lastly, he pleaded that a number of commitments had been made to other people, including the former Governor and members of the technical committee. In all, half of the 2% was already promised.

All this fell on deaf ears and the new Governor, smiling, insisted that 2% *was* possible and that it should be paid to him as soon as the contract was won and payments were received by the businessman. Even an offer to bring about a meeting between His

Highness and the representatives of the Swedish company was refused. The options of the Saudi businessman were clear: either he gave the 2% to the Prince, and paid the others involved a few million dollars out of his own pocket, or he fought it out at the risk of losing the deal, the goodwill of that particular Prince and perhaps the goodwill of the whole Saudi Royal Family, and be reduced to a position where he could no longer operate.

The businessman was and is wealthy. He could afford to pay the out-of-pocket expenses and other commissions. He could afford to pay more, and when the Swedes finalised the deal he took that option. Bitterly he considered it an investment in the future and particularly in his relationship with the new Governor.

Of all the stories I know about intermediary and skimming activities in the Middle East, the strangest one is that of President Saddam Hussein of Iraq. He is a benevolent skimmer. He does not act for himself, or for members of his families or his cronies. He acts for the benefit of his generals (known cynically as his unknown soldiers) – without their knowledge and very often without their approval.

Saddam Hussein is a firm believer in two maxims: first, that people with full bellies don't make revolutions, which doesn't concern us here, and second that corrupt generals do not overthrow governments. Believing this, President Hussein very often lets it be known to companies supplying his army with material that he wishes the generals connected with various projects to receive a fee or commission. It is never a direct request; the President has his ways of transmitting the message. At one time he entrusted the job to his Palestinian intellectual sidekick, who was very much party to this peculiar line of thinking.

I know of two occasions, one involving a French aircraft company, one the British helicopter manufacturer Westland, where President Hussein's trusty Palestinian suggested that they pay the generals concerned with their product a certain sum. In both cases the companies agreed. In the French case, a lone general, a professional soldier with an impeccable record, a man who had loyally served the monarchy as well as the republic, a traditionalist, totally disinterested in politics, declined the offer to his everlasting credit. I am told on good authority that this man owes a hefty mortgage on his house on the Tigris in Baghdad. All the other generals succumbed.

In one small Arab state, which is suspicious of its neighbours and which therefore maintains a considerable military establishment, an interesting case of institutional skimming has arisen. Most of the business transacted in this country concerns the supply of hardware and other material to the armed forces, and two people consider themselves the rightful beneficiary of commissions on these deals – the Head of State and the Minister of Defence who are, unsurprisingly, close relatives.

The Head of State's gang – he is surrounded by former British Army officers – goes on the prowl whenever a sizeable arms deal is in the making. Their job is easy when the agent involved is just a local merchant, but the situation becomes extremely delicate when they find, as is very often the case, that the deal concerns none other than the Minister of Defence, their boss's relative. For years they were reluctant to explain the problem to their chief, and pretended that failures were due to companies' refusal to co-operate with them. When one of them finally explained the problem, that most of these companies were represented by his relative, the Head of State snapped back that the Minister of Defence was to be treated like all other people. This meant that his own representatives could impose themselves on a company working with the Minister of Defence; a case of skimmer versus skimmer.

Normal skimming situations are difficult enough. A situation between the number one and the number two man in any country is almost impossible for companies to decipher. What adds to the difficulty is the Head of State's personal disinclination to contact any company directly. Thus companies have to rely on the word of an emissary expatriate Englishman, against that of the Minister of Defence himself, the chief's relative. Much to the chagrin of some government suppliers, such as the US Government, many a major deal to equip this country with arms and prepare it to face the surrounding dangers, have been delayed for months at a time, while the Head of State and his mates apply pressure on a company until it agrees to pay them either in addition to, or part of, the commission being paid to the Minister of Defence.

*   *   *

The third type of skimmer is the bureaucrat skimmer and here the deals are smaller. Most of the time, this is the already mentioned member of a technical or special committee who can disqualify an offer, delay it or favour a competitor in his assessment. He doesn't dare oppose a powerful institutional skimmer or well-connected rover, so his sphere of operation is confined to projects too small for them.

One head of the Central Traders Committee of the United Arab Emirates is an inventive wizard. He has disqualified companies because their offers do not meet the requirements of the Arab Boycott Office, the body entrusted with seeing that companies close to Israel are kept out. The rules of this body are vague, so he has ample room to manoeuvre. He has questioned an offer's adherence to specifications, turned down electrical equipment from Korea because it was 'unsafe' and claimed an offer didn't arrive in time, when it did. When he is bought into friendly behaviour, he tells his collaborators who their competitors are and the contents of their offers.

Bureaucrat skimmers are a fixture of Middle East business. Unlike institutional skimmers, they have to be extremely careful. Their position is important but far from unassailable.

Skimming has become prevalent. One could make a case that all the members of the House of Saud are involved in it. So are the major ministers and sheikhs in other countries. It is easy in countries where the skimmer is a permanent fixture, a prince or a sheikh, and his status doesn't change. The difficulty arises in dealing with ministers or bureaucrats who could lose their portfolio any day. Sometimes ministers are dropped from a cabinet after they have secured part of a deal. Whoever replaces them wants to skim as well. This raises the commission level because too many people are acting as skimmers rather than intermediaries.

The institutional, roving and bureaucrat skimmer are extensions of the intermediary business. Not all intermediary deals involve skimmers, but they are never too far away and the tempting size of a deal can create one instantly.

4

Spheres of Influence in East and West

An appreciation of power and influence and their sources is an indispensable sixth sense to an intermediary. He contends with two different spheres of power: the one in total control in the Middle East and the checks and balances and more segmented power system in the West and some parts of the Far East. These differences plague the intermediary and make his job one of the most intriguing in the world.

To the intermediary the Middle East government, ruler and money are one, and this combination is the ultimate arbiter of his success or failure. It produces effects by little-understood, invisible means. All other sources are tributary and should be judged by how they stand in relation to the government-ruler-money combination.

It is true that billionaires exist in Kuwait and Saudi Arabia. They wield considerable influence with government circles and have diversified their investments and sources of income on an international scale. Nonetheless, their power base within their country is totally dependent upon their relationship to their ruler. Without being in the good graces of the government/ruler, they are ineffectual in business. This is also why the rulers are always the wealthiest people.

As we have already seen (Chapter 3), one of the leading businessmen in Saudi Arabia, Garish Mabrouk, lost influence overnight because he offended the Crown Prince Fahd. Similarly, the number one arms dealer in Jordan was shunted aside by Premier Abdel Hamid Sharraf (undoubtedly the Mr Clean of modern Arab politics) and did not recover until after the latter's untimely death in 1981. Many Iraqi political exiles are extremely competent, but totally impotent because they are out of favour with the present government. Former Saudi oil minister Abdullah Al Tariki, a co-founder of OPEC, is considered by many to be a man of exceptional brilliance with more substance and less glitter than the present oil minister, Zaki Yamani, but he is reduced to accepting jobs as an advisor in Libya and Algeria, and lives off his salary. He's not short of money, but his situation must be frustrating. The man has had no power base since he alienated the Saudi Royal Family by foolishly trying to fashion a personal oil policy and was consequently forced into exile.

It is also the ruler who grants preferential treatment to one country, company or person and denies it to another, has final say about his country's list of priorities and divides his country's pie among friends and followers in what he considers the surest way to perpetuate control by his own dynasty or group. There are no checks on his power. King Fahd's pocket and the state treasury are one and the same. So the intermediary must form a view on the political direction of the country, maintain the relationship between his group and the ruler, and fully understand the latter's attitude towards keeping himself in power by distributing money to his followers (which determines who gets what).

The spheres of power and influence in the West are organised ones which determine the behaviour of companies and individuals. They too start at government level, but change as they move down the line because government involvement in the everyday conduct of business is limited by the laws of the land and commitment to a free enterprise system.

These laws can prohibit involvement in intermediary-type activity; this is particularly the case in the US, with its anti-corruption laws, Security and Exchange Commission investigations, and general policy of monitoring and checking questionable payments. The laws in the West exempt no one, not even Prince Bernhard of Holland or former Premier Tanaka of Japan. Even British Prime Minister's son Mark Thatcher has been hounded by the press. Like Middle Eastern laws or systems, Western ones are an extension of social and cultural attitudes. The Middle East's 'giving and receiving' wealth-distribution formula leads to commissions for intermediaries. The West frowns on and sometimes forbids them.

Western governments can and do impose limitations on the export of strategic goods – the most obvious example being arms. But their policies also affect the availability of export credit and other incentives to companies dealing in non-strategic goods. The intermediary must bear in mind what help or hindrance a government is likely to offer when selecting the right company for the right project.

He must also understand the laws of a country and national corporate attitudes. Laws are slow to change, even though government attitudes may alter overnight with a new administration. The US Government, for instance, may very well wish to facilitate the involvement of American companies in Middle East development schemes; but there are laws on the books forbidding the payment of commissions. This effectively rules out any chance of a US company landing a big contract. I have no doubt that some US officials would dearly like to find a way round this anti-corruption law.

In Chapter 2 we looked at the countries of the Middle East from the point of view of an outside businessman who wishes to enter the market. The Arabs, however, have their own view of foreigners tendering for contracts and the intermediary must always keep these in mind. The attitude of Arabs to various nationalities, and vice versa, can give or deny consent to the most elaborate plans by an intermediary. Corporate attitudes – national ones with a business front – come into this.

For example, good intermediaries are very leery about using the Japanese and South Koreans to supply goods or equipment, because they pay little attention to delivery dates. South Korea, furthermore, has a spotty record in the area of quality control. On the other hand, these nationalities are preferred for bricks-and-mortar construction projects because they can easily obtain cheap, hard-working labour. Besides, both the Japanese and South Korean Governments have their overt and covert ways of subsidising their companies to give them a competitive edge over their Western counterparts. The bigger the construction project the truer this is. (The South Koreans use their soldiers as labourers. As they are already paid by the government their wages consist of the expense of getting them to Saudi Arabia, etc.)

The major stumbling block impeding co-operation with the South Koreans and Japanese is their 'foreignness' to people in the Middle East. The ways of Western people are more sympathetic to an Arab and the regimentation of the Oriental is very offensive to the Arab's sense of individualism. In other words, while an Arab business view of the Japanese and South Korean may be positive, the personal one is negative. As business is a highly personal affair, this is a crucial distinction with obvious results.

Similarly, the Japanese and South Korean view of the Arab is less than complimentary. The Arab lack of a sense of time is a particular source of annoyance. Another is the lack of uniformity in the Arab's behaviour which leaves the stiff Orientals at a loss as to how to respond. Last, but not least, in this list of difficulties is the Arab's racial consciousness which places the Oriental behind his Western equals. With little or no appreciation for Oriental ways, the Arab tends to view the Japanese and South Koreans as true foreigners when compared with Western people, whom he knows better.

Whether they admit it or not, there is an implicit bond between the Germans and the Arabs: their historic attitude towards the Jews. Seldom, if ever, is this spoken of openly but it provides the background against which their relationship functions.

The Germans are held to be efficient and businesslike, the creators of superior quality products, the subscribers to deadlines and achievers of the impossible; in others words, a bit of the superman image lingers in the Arab mind. Sadly, Arab admiration for the German is not reciprocated by the latter, who sees the Arab as an unavoidable accident with whom he has to contend and accords him to higher racial standing than the Israeli or African, both of whom he considers inferior. Everything the Arab stands for is anathema to the German and it is the Arab who must make the running.

Mercedes trucks are the largest sellers in the Middle East in spite of their almost forbidding price tag – $80,000 for the smaller ones.

The German construction company Wyess and Freytag makes it plain that their prices are likely to be higher than competitors', while modestly saying 'but we do a better job'. German cosmetics sell at a premium throughout the Middle East, although their long brand names escape the inelegant pronunciation of most Arabs.

The German is neither bound nor limited by laws or regulations against using intermediaries, nor do moral scruples stand in the way. He views working with Arabs as a necessary evil and believes that whatever might be corruption in Western terms reflects more on the Arabs than himself. His personal behaviour perpetuates the aura of Mr Clean, for he neither gives nor receives presents and is never familiar enough to want to be part of any deal on a personal basis. Simply stated, the German is out to do business in accordance with his own superior ways. He succeeds because the Arab believes that his arrogance is justified.

If independence is the hallmark of German business then its absence is characteristic of the French. Nowhere is the uniformity, the oneness, of government and business approach so apparent as it is with the French. Their government fronts for business. Like their politicians, French businessmen are crude, hard-knuckles salesmen who are not reluctant to play dirty. The French made more of the showing of the film *Death of a Princess* on British and American television than anyone else. They pointed to it as an example of Anglo-American anti-Arab bias. They are open in their references to their government support for the Arabs against Israel and to the American espousal of Israeli causes.

The French opinion of the Arab is no different from their view of everyone else: the whole world is out of step except the French. On the other hand, the Arabs' assessment of them is a combination of affection and fear. They see them as warm Mediterranean people like themselves, believers in accommodation, petty and slippery at moments while totally reliable at others. Certainly they have a more instinctive understanding of Middle Eastern wheeling and dealing than do their German, Oriental or Anglo-Saxon competitors.

*   *   *

If they ever had to classify the people with whom they work, the Arabs would place the British at the bottom of the scale, though they have been in the Middle East longest. They resent what they consider British arrogance, are impatient with their slow business methods, dislike their personal attitudes and are outspoken in their accusation of laziness. Conversely, the British cannot get over their past colonial hang-ups, are full of derision towards Arab ways and manage to appear disinterested even when they are not.

For reasons too complex to list, the British appear to take longer to make a decicion than most people, be it at government, company or individual level. It is easier for me, based in London, to get an answer from Germany or the US than from a British company two streets away. As a result, their share of the booming Middle East construction market has declined in every Middle Eastern country, their share of the automobile and truck business is non-existent and even traditional redoubts such as textiles have been hit hard by Far Eastern competitors. Not to mention the conspicuous absence of British industry in areas such as consumer electronics, household products and foods. British technology is at an intermediate stage, neither advanced and thus necessary nor cheap and hence attractive.

The two areas where British industry continues to perform satisfactorily are whisky and arms sales. Black Label whisky outsells all other spirits throughout the Middle East – even in countries like Saudi Arabia, where it has to be smuggled in. Also, in spite of bitter sniping at French amorality, the British have sold armament and supporting equipment to the UAE, Oman, Qatar, Jordan, Iraq and Egypt (Westland Helicopters, Racal, Plessey Electronics, British Aerospace) and they have even offered bridges for military use (made by Fairey Engineering) to Libya in the middle of that country's invasion of Chad.

There is a love-hate relationship between the Arabs and the British. British attitudes are a known entity in the Middle East because they have been there longer and many Arabs genuinely wish to see greater British commitment to the region. But their unjustified self-righteousness is resented and so is their lack of get-up-and-go.

*   *   *

Nowhere is there a greater dichotomy between the attitude towards the individual and towards the government than in the Arab's attitude towards America. Arabs love American openness, lack of complexity and straight talk. The American may very well harbour feelings of prejudice towards the black but no such feelings exist towards the Arab nor is there a questionable colonial tradition.

It is for the pro-Israeli American Government that the Arab reserves his harsh words. Whether it is a reflection of real feeling or the usual Arab lip service, Arabs do go to great pains to distinguish between the American and his government, particularly in the presence of individual Americans.

Amazingly, Arabs have a secret admiration for American anti-corruption laws. Though they keep many American companies from participating in tenders, they reflect positively on what the Arabs consider American honesty. The American presence is enhanced through their association with services business and their ability to plan and organise. Now that building and equipping are well on their way, the need for maintenance is growing. Waste Management Inc cleans the streets of Riyadh and the US Corp of Engineers has been in Saudi Arabia overseeing major construction projects for over thirty years.

American industry and the American's ability to undertake work are not separate from each other. To the Arab, Americans may do work of only average quality but they are able to undertake large projects and they have a sense of organisation which the Arab would like to emulate. Whatever business organisations exist in the Middle East have an American hue to them.

Apart from governments, laws, national and corporate attitudes, the intermediary must consider the strengths and weaknesses of individual corporations. This is harder to tackle since intermediaries are not, by nature, a studious lot. However, increased competition has forced many an intermediary to examine the performance of many corporations in an attempt to match more accurately the right company with the right job.

To sum up, an intermediary has to contend with an elaborate structure of influence on both sides of the fence. There is the

Middle East government ruler, his control of money, and his relationship to the intermediary, which is superimposed upon the body politic of the country and the need of the ruling classes to perpetuate their control. Then there is the attitude of the Western government, its laws, the inherent national attitudes and the corporate constraints, likes and dislikes. In all it makes for an awesome set of requirements which very few people can master. Certainly there is more to being an intermediary than people may think, and the demands upon his talents become more stringent every day.

5

Uncommon Grounds Between East and West

Concluding a conventional business deal in the West presupposes the existence of basic ingredients which are missing in concluding deals in the Middle East. Western businessmen view a deal as a *business* method of legally apportioning or sharing in the benefits of a transaction common to a number of participants. Their Middle East counterparts see it as a *private*, individual arrangement producing profits – but not subject to or regulated by more than the whims of the parties involved.

First of all, West and East do not speak the same language, either in the wider sense, as a means to ordinary communication, or the narrower one of using business terms which mean the same to both parties. The Western businessman is aware of and feels bound by the laws and regulations bearing on a deal. He expects a formal commitment in writing, and discretion in handling privileged information; he operates on the basis of sophisticated financial analysis involving profit and loss projections, and assumes there is a mutuality of interest between the parties involved.

It is not easy for people from such different cultures to understand each other even in everyday conversation. And the gap in communication is more marked when East and West must arrive at common meanings for over-used business terms like agent, representative, partner and joint venture.

A Western corporation may think of an agent or representative as being one of many with whom it co-operates, while the agent

61

himself may think the word assigns him the exclusive right to represent the company. This can happen when both sides fail to be explicit and precise enough about what they mean by agent. It can also happen by design, when the agent wants to elevate himself to a more rewarding financial position. As in domestic matters, the word partner means different things to different people. Middle East traders interpret it as anyone with whom they do or have done business, whereas the Western meaning is more exact, suggesting sharing of the equity of a company and/or its benefits. Most abused is the phrase 'joint venture', which can cover anything from informally co-operating on a single venture to forming a joint stock company on a permanent basis. A Westerner must insist on exact definitions from the start.

This insistence should apply also to the use of local laws and regulations (when they exist and are adequate). Only official translations should be accepted. Also, it should be remembered that these laws are enacted to protect the local people and their interests and should be viewed that way, otherwise the chances of misunderstanding and misinterpretation are increased dramatically and unnecessarily. Instances of local traders twisting a translation around to favour their position are legend. In Kuwait, an outside company cannot make an offer to a government department without having a local agent. The Kuwaiti law means an agent for that particular offer. However, local traders use the existence of the law to tie up outside companies on a permanent basis.

Second to using a language understood by all parties, comes the matter of the legality of the transaction. In the West, the legal acceptability of any deal under consideration by reputable corporations or people is taken for granted. Deals are stopped in their tracks when people suffer from fears as to their 'legality' in whole or in part. Regardless of what a deal concerns, its size, or what its results are supposed to be, it will have to subscribe to the word of the law or an acceptable interpretation thereof.

In the Middle East, the legality or otherwise of a deal may not be an issue. There are multitudes of situations not covered by existing laws and there are many others where the word of the law is vague. For example, the extremely important proviso of submitting disputes to an International Chamber of Commerce for arbitration may be nothing more than hot air in Saudi Arabia, since there is no way a Moslem judge would subordinate the Koranic word to that of a Swiss, Dutch or any other abitrator. This is particularly true of banking laws where the word of the Koran is relatively clear and is in direct conflict with modern banking practice. Written Libyan laws are totally irrelevant because everything in that country depends on the whim of Colonel Qaddafi who is as unpredictable as a spring storm. Yemeni import laws regarding what constitute luxury items are so inexact they depend on the ability of the importer to convince the customs man of his point of view. More importantly, the local agent is dismissive of any legal constraints placed on the company. Very few agents respect US anti-corruption laws forbidding the use of funds to bribe a government official, etc. They think there must be a way around them.

So, laws can be non-existent or vague. For the sophisticated, they do not present obstacles; they can be circumvented, through bribery or by simply ignoring them. An important Emirates person wishing to build a new office block on a piece of land slated to become a beautification zone could either bribe the responsible official to change the boundaries of the zone or have him look the other way while he built inside the designated area. Shipments of whisky reach members of the House of Saud in shampoo sachets with the full knowledge of the local customs inspectors. This has prompted a businessman friend of mine to say, 'In Saudi Arabia, first came the label.'

In most Middle East countries, the pace with which laws are being enacted and amended leads to pleas of ignorance of the law – an acceptable excuse. The laws governing the formation of a joint venture company in the Yemen are changing so often, you can work under whichever suits you. All you have to do is to pay the concerned official to affix the suitable date on the document of the formation of the joint venture. This isn't easy, but it isn't difficult either.

In the West, putting everything in writing rests on belief in the laws regulating what is being done. It makes sense because the laws are adequate. In the Middle Ease, not only are the laws lacking or vague, the people don't believe in them. In other words, it is very hard to put together a legally binding document or write or speak in a language which reflects legal commitment, because the legal framework of Middle Eastern countries isn't sufficiently developed and even when it is, people have a natural aversion to it. When I complained to a Kuwaiti lawyer about a clause in an agreement he drew up to cover a deal with a local company he told me not to waste time as 'the whole thing isn't worth the paper it's written on. They are big and powerful and if they don't want to honour the agreement, they won't.'

The Arab reluctance to lock oneself into exact situations goes beyond legal documents, and applies to everyday communications. Middle Eastern businessmen would rather not take a specific position, whether negative or positive. They are accustomed to things changing and believe rigid positions interfere with their ability to manoeuvre which, to them, is the most important aspect of doing business. Manoeuvring could mean anything from overcoming closing dates for public tenders to making false claims regarding a local company's ability to undertake part of the work in question.

A Saudi businessman proudly told me that his company didn't have a single written agreement with the various Western corporations with which he worked. He relied on verbal gentlemen's agreements, had enough power to cause the companies trouble if they misbehaved, and negotiated each deal separately because no two were the same. Besides, dealing with inexact and changing situations is much more exciting than dealing with known entities and it affords him freedom.

The question of whether a corporation considers someone its representative or not is critical and should be watched carefully. The number of companies who answer our queries on this subject with 'not really' is too numerous to list. 'Not really' leads to complications. Occasionally we take it to mean the corporation is free to work with us, which proves untrue and troublesome. Conversely, we sometimes take it to mean they are committed, which isn't true and opportunities are missed. Here the company can be the guilty party because 'not really' may mean waiting to see who can do a better job on a specific project then dropping the other party.

Generally speaking, Arabs are indiscreet. Secrecy – to abide by the law, protect one's business or out of politeness – is very seldom observed. The reasons for this are many, including the belief in speaking of wealth and influence, the smallness of business communities in all Middle East countries, absence of legal restraints and total lack of awareness of any adverse results indiscretion might cause. After all, there are no regulatory agencies or Security and Exchange Commission to investigate, nor are there stocks and shares to manipulate. It goes further; indiscretion can be part of a deliberate attempt to undermine or frustrate competitors. If you spread a rumour that a certain minister promised you a contract then your competitors are either discouraged or spend days finding out the truth.

I have previously mentioned the practice of boasting about money and success, to breed more. This sort of boasting happens in quieter ways, too. When I asked a Kuwaiti businessman what our chances of getting a deal were, he winked at me. This, to the experienced, is supposed to be an assurance that he had found a way of handling the situation in terms of the influence required to push it across the line. A Saudi associate invariably answers my queries about projects by smiling and getting that twinkle in his eye which always means there are ways of doing what needs to be done. He, too, feels he has found the key.

In the Middle East, just as in the industrial countries, the profit motive is the primary one in business deals. But most Arabs don't have the know-how to analyse the prospects and possible profits of a projected deal; nor is it possible for the most efficient Western company to draw up a proper forecast. The necessary information isn't there, and can't be guessed at with sufficient accuracy.

Contrary to common belief, there is an abundance of certain types of statistics on the Middle East – for example, what people buy and where it comes from. This is because most Middle Eastern countries import everything, and a little bit of digging produces all the needed data. When it comes to this type of information, Saudi Arabia may very well be the most widely researched country in the world. All one has to do is examine the records of the harbour and airport authorities and you get the total picture.

What is not available is reliable data on which one can act, not in the market place but on market dynamics. Putting it in plain words, it is the future size of a market and the behaviour of the consumers within it that make forecasting well-nigh impossible. This is so for various reasons, including the constant flow of first-time users of any product – cars, refrigerators, perfumes – the upward-mobility pressures which create such quirks as the average Kuwaiti family changing furniture every two years to keep up with the Abdullahs next door (Saudi Arabia's furniture market is bigger than the UK's), and the conversion of buyers of generic products into buyers of brand names, not to mention the ability of the consumer to articulate his needs, or to speak to women. Until recently, the Saudis, Kuwaitis, Omanis and Emirates people, even the Jordanians, bought perfume without attention to or knowledge of brand names. Now they have developed attachments to Christian Dior, Yves St Laurent and other designer labels. (The attendant at a London chemist misunderstood a Saudi lady's pronunciation and sent her to a liquor store to pick up Dewar's whisky instead of Dior perfume.)

Not being able to judge the direction of a market place is tantamount to not being able to judge what you can sell, making financial planning impossible. This applies not only to consumer products, but to industrial products as well. The market for cheap prefab building units for expatriate labourers collapsed when construction companies throughout the Middle East began using discarded shipping containers instead. Some trading companies lost millions of dollars in inventory. People have formed joint ventures to manufacture metal building sections which go into aeroplane hangars and storage sheds, only to discover they are cheaper to import from Italy, Greece and even the UK because this is a labour-intensive enterprise and labour in those countries is considerably cheaper than imported labour in Saudi Arabia. The supply-demand situation for hotel rooms is the exact opposite of what it was years ago when people slept in taxis because hotels overbooked. Nowadays visitors make fewer trips to an expensive Middle East and many of them stay with their business associates. Most hotels are half empty, there is a price war in the making and what, until recently, looked like an attractive investment area, has turned into a financial disaster for most hotel owners.

As these examples demonstrate, Western-type financial analysis is not possible and reliance on entrepreneurial judgement rather than figures is necessary. Developing a pay-out schedule for any product or service is impossible. The unpredictability of market dynamics is matched by the unpredictability of governments and their changing list of priorities; and even the laws which govern the conduct of business change so often they can turn attractive situations into financially unrewarding ones.

The all-embracing mutuality of interest may not be present when East and West meet. This mutuality of interest is supposed to occur at two stages in the West: it is the thing that brings people together and it determines their behaviour afterwards.

In the West this interest is financial. All other elements are secondary. This is not so in the Middle East, where a company will enter into agreements with you to keep you from competitors or for strictly prestige purposes – the plaque on the door. After a relationship is established Middle East businessmen have been known to pursue projects for fun and publicity purposes, as a decoy for some of their other activities or as spoilers, to muddy the waters for people they don't like. No wonder some sedate Western companies think their Middle East representatives, partners or associates to be crazy camel jockeys who must be kept under constant check.

With such major differences glaringly obvious, how can a Western corporation set about realising its share of this potentially lucrative market? Are there checks and balances it can employ to avoid the sometimes fatal trial-and-error system used at present?

One fact is unalterable, regardless of the type of company, product or service under consideration: the Middle East is not and will not be capable of supplying the marketing and legal framework for the conduct of business in the traditional Western way for many years to come – if ever. This fact must be accepted from the outset and a decision to live with the difficulties it creates must be made early in the game.

Still, beating the people of the Middle East at their own game is not particularly difficult. Western companies should always play hard to get – this makes them more attractive to a would-be Middle East suitor. All agreements should be made in writing regardless of whether the other side likes it or not. This point should never be negotiable. Even when the laws concerned are not enforceable they should be used as a guideline. All agreements should be made volumetric and term agreements. The first part forces people to work and the second provides a way out in case things don't happen. Agreements should state exactly what the Western company expects to realise, and should avoid delving into a sharing of profits, etc., because the local man will run circles round you. What would one say if he said he used half the profits to bribe a minister?

Unless we are dealing with an exceptionally effective outfit, everything should be done at the start to create a state of 'friendly tension'. This means maintaining an amicable but distant relationship implying an unpredictability which keeps Middle East associates on their toes. This should last until a company and its services or products are accepted to such an extent that the associate is forced to pay careful attention to mutual interests. A state of friendly tension will not alienate your associate. On the contrary, it will endear you to him. It is a game he understands.

There are many ways of keeping this air of unpredictability at the early stages of an association, including constant nagging about sundry pieces of business as well as flooding the associate with bits and pieces of news about what the competition is doing. And you can always show up unannounced and conduct what amounts to an inspection tour.

Once business has been transacted the relationship develops its own momentum, superceding doubt and misunderstanding. Whatever was done to effect business becomes the term of reference, and it is usually an amalgam of Western and Eastern ways.

6

———— •◦• ————

Never the Twain

The culture gap is, of course, the single biggest obstacle to doing business in the Middle East. Most non-Arabs simply do not understand enough about the area and its inhabitants to succeed there.

This lack of understanding afflicts West-Arab political relations and business overall, as well as intermediary-effected business. Using an intermediary to co-ordinate a transaction does not necessarily overcome the cultural barrier. On the contrary, because one deals with a greater number of people, the possibilities for making mistakes are increased.

There are individual mistakes and there are ones with a national identity, more likely to be committed by a specific national group. The Japanese and the Koreans are known to over-promise and not fulfil, but the Arabs do the same. Some Americans carry their folksy relaxation and desire to please to absurd lengths. One joined me in visiting a Kuwaiti business friend and saw us greet each other with the traditional kiss on both cheeks. Next time he saw my Kuwaiti associate, the American hugged and kissed him for several embarrassing minutes.

Still, there is no definite pattern, so I will simply tell a number of stories as representative and amusing examples of cultural cross-currents which interfere with the proper conduct of business. They are all true, all bordering on the absurd, all reflecting problems of misunderstanding between outside businessmen and people in the Middle East. All the stories involve the intermediary, and poignantly point up the delicate nature of his job. Imagine a

Korean and a Saudi finalising a business contract, when neither has a good command of English.

There is nothing anyone can do in an hour, a day, a week, even a month, to prepare any businessman, whatever his background, for what will confront him in the Middle East. He is on his own there. He needs a social antenna, a particular sensitivity to keep himself, the company he represents, his intermediary and his intermediary's boss out of trouble. Sensitivity of this nature depends on understanding Middle Eastern culture or responding to it in an acceptable way – preferably both.

For one thing, contradictory though it may appear, while Arabs totally accept that business is done by purchasing influence, it is an unspoken acceptance. Everyone concerned may know perfectly well that a sheikh or minister is involved in a pay-off, but it is worse than gross bad manners to mention his name. My first story concerns Iraq, where there is a law against using intermediaries. It is freqently and flagrantly broken – but no one ever admits that in words.

My associate in Iraq (my Mr Big) requested a company to make an offer to the Iraqi Government for 300,000 tons of rolled steel for building purposes. He expressed preference for a Japanese or Korean company because he thought their prices would be lower. On the basis of an elementary investigation my findings supported his view but the quantity required proved too big for the Koreans. The Japanese could meet the Iraqis' needs and we proceeded to work with one of their companies, trying to help them beat their Western competitors.

The London office of a major Japanese trading company agreed to a payment of 3% to me and my associates on the total value of the contract when the business had been transacted. From this 3% all types of government supporters had to be 'covered', but as it was a sizeable order, there was enough to go around.

In accordance with our instructions, the company wrote to the Iraqi Ministry of Housing expressing an interest in making an offer. They enclosed the usual brochures and lists of supply of projects which they had successfully completed as well as an indication of price. Our people within government circles arranged for an invitation to be issued to an executive of the Japanese company to visit Baghdad, to begin negotiating the awarding of this contract.

The delegate chosen was a member of their London office management. He and I met five times so that I could brief him on conditions in Iraq and explain how he should behave in the presence of local officialdom. The most important and delicate matter was to convey to him our thoughts on the lower echelons of government bureaucracy. The first people he was likely to meet at the Ministry of Housing were not decision-makers, knew very little about the contract itself and nothing about our 'arrangement'. They would, I advised him, subject him to the usual bureaucratic questioning and small bothers. Behaving like this makes them feel important. I added more information about the decision-makers, 'our people', but advised that they should never be spoken of directly. Nor, I continued, should he ever speak of us at all because he was already known to the important people in Iraq and they would facilitate the successful completion of his mission. My last briefing to him cautioned repeatedly against using our name and advised that he be equipped with the maximum amount of patience to meet the inevitable awaiting him at the hands of the lowly bureaucrats. All my advice was accepted by the usual nod of the Oriental head.

The Japanese businessman's Iraqi visa was obtained and he proceeded to Baghdad a week later. As expected, he was confronted by a rather difficult bureaucrat who wanted to know all about him, his company, his offer and even his country. Unfortunately for all concerned this process took longer than usual – three days. This appeared to tax the patience of our Japanese friend who finally lost his temper and demanded a meeting with his tormentor's immediate superior. This was – to our surprise – instantaneously arranged.

Stomping into the office of the second Iraqi official, all my painstaking briefings and preparations forgotten, he complained about his treatment, particularly in view of the promise made to him that the contract was his for the asking. When asked who made this promise, he not only named me but also one of my associates. The senior Iraqi official looked at him in utter amazement and answered, 'Believe me, I have never heard of them, nor is any one entitled to make promises in the name of the Iraqi government. The only thing I can do is to take you to the Deputy Minister himself.'

A meeting with the Deputy Minister was arranged. He was one of 'our people' and he was fully aware of who I was and who my associate was. He had been waiting for the Japanese gentleman to reach him, but not under the present circumstances. He met the Japanese gentleman in the presence of his subordinates and heard the man repeat his complaint.

The Deputy Minister was utterly shocked by his visitor's indiscretion. Luckily for us all there was no loss of nerve. Instead the Deputy Minister looked at his subordinates and declared in Arabic that he too had never heard either of myself or of my associate and that the whole thing must be a hoax.

He then apologised to the Japanese gentleman and told him the Iraqi Government's laws forbade intermediary activity and that reputable Japanese companies such as his should never, under any circumstances, associate themselves with something illegal. The awarding of this contract, he added, would have to go through the normal procedures and take the normal amount of time. This meant three months from then and the immediate future offered little, if any, possibility of change. The conclusion was another mild apology and the gentlemen shook hands and parted company.

Later, the Deputy Minister summoned his subordinates for a private meeting. He described the incident as very bad; it could lead to scandal, and it excluded the Japanese company from competition. Their error was too great to be forgiven, according to him. He labelled his Japanese visitor a troublemaker, who should be referred to the Ministry of the Interior. Slowly, meticulously, he secured the approval of his subordinates to expel the man from Iraq immediately because he was indulging in a forbidden activity, the use of an intermediary. In their presence he telephoned the police, told them what had happened and advised that the man be immediately deported from Iraq.

The Iraqi police, not the gentlest people under the best circumstances, rushed into the Baghdad Hotel, practically carried blabbermouth out by the elbows and booked him on the first plane for London. He arrived at Heathrow eight hours later and, even before leaving the airport, telephoned me to ask what had happened.

What had happened in Baghdad had already been transmitted to me in code. I knew the story well. My answer to the Japanese gentleman was to ask him to refrain from contacting my office. We had no wish to work with him or his company. I would only explain things to his superiors in person in my office. They did come to see me. The situation was explained to them and the young man was transferred back to Japan and away from international business in ten days.

My second example of a cultural difference making business impossible is unique. In this case, the about-to-be beneficiary, an American contractor, turned down a sure piece of business because he didn't like Arab ways. I journeyed to Riyadh, in Saudi Arabia, to meet Prince Mishawi bin Ahmad who was interested in building a shopping centre. My companion was the president of a company which specialised in building shopping centres in the States and Canada.

We had established contact with the Prince through his aide-de-camp. His interest in a Riyadh shopping centre was high, though he was unequipped to support his assessment of its potential with any statistics. His aide, who introduced us to the project, had agreed to share our commission of 4%. We had received the necessary written confirmation of the Prince's intentions, of the availability of a piece of land, and of $12,000,000 to $14,000,000 for the buildings.

The contract with the American company was established on the basis of the Prince's letter of intent. I met with the president in London and obtained the – always needed – agreement to pay us 4%. Then we travelled to Riyadh.

On our first day there, we were subjected to lavish traditional hospitality by the Prince's aide. Intermittently we were given little titbits of information about the Prince, assured that he was a good fellow and serious businessman and advised of his likes and dislikes.

Finally, to the meeting with the Prince himself. To look at, Prince Mishawi was a very attractive young man, about thirty years old. As suspected, he was unprepared to discuss the project either conceptually or on any business terms known to us. The desire was there and so was the money. We met in a huge room, full of uncomfortable chairs and persian carpets, with bare, white walls whose monotony was broken by an occasional gold object, such as a dagger, a sword, an incense burner. The room was part of a compound of four houses surrounded by a huge cement wall. The Prince, dressed in traditional Saudi dish-dash and sandals, kept addressing himself to the American, exercising his knowledge of the innumerable Arabic words for welcome, adding, 'Mr Ross, you must do this for me.'

Mr Ross was willing. Building shopping centres was Mr Ross's speciality. But Mr Ross, while being subjected to all the pleasantries, was being subjected to two other things the like of which he hadn't even seen in the movies. As he spoke, the Prince, having kicked off his sandals, was massaging the toes of his foot with one hand and picking his nose with the other. Mr Ross hid his disgust and kept nodding and agreeing with everything the Prince said. After many cups of coffee and tea we left the royal presence to be driven back to our hotel by the Prince's leg-man.

Characteristically, the leg-man had stayed behind a minute or two to speak to the Prince. They always have on-the-spot conferences no matter how rude it appears. I used this opportunity to quiz Mr Ross about his view of the project. Enthusiastically I added, 'We've got it if we want it.' I will never forget the answer: 'No, I don't want it.' When I asked why, he said, 'He is an ignorant young man. Imagine what he would have been doing if he had a third hand. My friend, I can't live with people like him. I don't need people like him to make a living. To hell with him and to hell with Saudi Arabia. It's not even a country, it's a building site with a few madmen wandering around.'

The head of the entertainment committee, the Prince's aide, continued to offer hospitality and I prevailed on Ross to stay in Riyadh for two more days to explore other opportunities. The day before we left, we were in Siteen Street in the middle of town as a taxi whizzed by, the driver making a huge racket with his horn. Siteen Street is a six-lane highway, three each way, and there was no traffic in sight. Mr Ross was amused; he couldn't see any reason for the driver to make so much noise. He was unacquainted with the Arabs' love for automobile horns.

A bit tongue-in-cheek and still trying to get over the débâcle of the previous day, I reminded him of the young man in Caldwell's *God's Little Acre* who would get into the lady preacher's car, honk the horn incessantly until he worked himself into a highly sexual state, then come out and show her a good time. He eventually married her. Mr Ross chuckled politely.

We drove to the airport next day down Siteen Street, the empty battleground for our horn-honking friend. Again, the street was empty, our driver was young and he honked his horn non-stop. For a moment Mr Ross's conventional propriety was forgotten; he jokingly threw his head on my shoulder and whispered, 'Friend, one of us is in trouble. This boy's working up to it.'

Mr Ross continues to be my friend, but he has never done business in Saudi Arabia. He rightly decided he couldn't live with the people.

There are occasions when officials of Arab countries visit the West to meet and assess companies wishing to work with them. The Iraqis do this more than any other country and, considering their strict laws, they do so in a very strange way. They actually accept all-expenses-paid invitiations. Their government condones such acceptance and looks the other way while the company pays for a first-class airline ticket and a posh hotel plus lavish entertainment.

We were party to one of these arrangements. An Iraqi Deputy Minister of Planning was invited to London to meet one of the major British contracting companies (Taylor Woodrow). This company was being considered for building a university, a huge project in an area where the company had much expertise. Taylor Woodrow issued the invitation when it became a 'finalist', one of three companies still in contention for the project. They thought it would be a good idea for him to see for himself examples of work they had done in this particular field.

We were very happy with the connection both with the Deputy Minister and this reputable corporation. We had organised the invitation; the ticket was despatched and the man arrived. I entertained him for the first twenty-four hours prior to his visit to a senior member of the company's board.

The following day we journeyed a little distance out of London to the company's headquarters. Our host was a man who knew the construction world, particularly in the Middle East and Iraq, and demonstrated considerable sensitivity to Arab business ways. For two hours he regaled our visiting dignitary with details about his company and the qualities which placed them ahead of the two competitors. This fine gentleman made one mistake before we left his office. Having invited us to dinner at his club in London he wanted the Minister to meet the company's resident expert on the Middle East and Iraq. The resident expert had been waiting for the summons. He walked into the boardroom in grey trousers, blazer, suede shoes and sporting a monocle. He was portly, with a bushy red moustache, and looked every inch the retired colonel that he was. He shook hands with our visitor, introduced himself and smiled politely.

The member of the board then gave his preamble, briefing his expert on what had transpired, and expressed the hope that he would join us for dinner later on. The expert was designated to go to Baghdad next to meet with the Deputy Minister and his staff for a thorough review of his company's offer. The preamble was a piece of professional wisdom: short, witty and wise.

Unfortunately, the expert on the Middle East and Iraq had his turn. After all, he was summoned for a purpose – to demonstrate his knowledge – and he supposedly had something to say. He turned to the Deputy Minister, monocle screwed tight in the eye, and said, 'I say, you come from Mesopotamia, do you? Know it well. Marched there in 1941 when some of your people misbehaved. With Slim, you know. Put it down in a few days – not great soldiers, your boys. Weren't then at least.'

The previously successful meeting closed disastrously and instead of confirming the date for dinner I promised the director I would call him back about it. We were driven back to the Grosvenor House Hotel in central London. The Deputy's only comment on the subject was, 'Mesopotamia, eh . . . even that son-of-a-bitch isn't that old. No one has called our country Mesopotamia for thousands of years and with the proper training I'd put any of our boys against theirs any time of the day. There is no way that I can work with this company.'

I must admit I didn't try to change his mind. Instead I telephoned the director who accepted what had happened and cancelled dinner. I advised them to withdraw the offer because they would be throwing good money after bad. I told him the Deputy Minister's Arab pride was upset and apologising to him would only make it worse. I have no idea where our expert on Mesopotamia ended up; he lost that job, but there are still companies ignorant enough about the Middle East to employ him.

Some taboos of Arab society are so well known that, when they are infringed by ignorant foreigners, I honestly find it hard to understand either how the individual can be so ill-informed or how his company can employ him on business abroad. A brief story about an Australian fellow will illustrate what I mean.

The drinking of alcohol is forbidden in Saudi Arabia. It is difficult for me to conceive of this fact being unknown to anyone in the world. It is also very difficult for me to conceive of any businessman who doesn't know that British Airways flights from London to Jeddah serve drinks while you are on board the aircraft until it enters Saudi air space. I have flown with British Airways many times and I enjoy a drink, and I have seen passengers have, perhaps, one too many – but no one goes over the top.

On one such trip, however, someone did. The guilty party was an Australian, a representative of a major Australian meat company, travelling first class to Saudi Arabia to promote his products. After all, Saudi Arabia imports more beef per capita than any other country in the world.

The Australian was drinking too much. The cabin staff cut him off. This proved to be a temporary interference because he opened his briefcase, produced a bottle of whisky and continued to drink. The supervisor of the cabin staff approached him and told him of the potentially disastrous result. His advise was ignored.

On that particular January day, we left London when the temperature was near freezing and arrived in Jeddah when the temperature was over 80°F. When we disembarked our friend's condition was made so much worse by the sudden blast of heat and desert sun that by the time he was inside the terminal he was hardly able to stand up. Not only that, but our arrival coincided with the afternoon Moslem prayers and the ground staff were lined up in three rows, pointing towards Mecca and paying their religious respects to the Holiest of Holies. Passengers on our flight stood only fifteen yards away from the praying figures, waiting for our luggage. Miraculously, the meat salesman made it through immigration.

It was a bizarre scene. There were about one hundred and eighty passengers who had arrived on the Lockheed 1011 huddled in a corner on one side, making every effort to avoid the Australian trespasser who was falling about on the other side of the unloading conveyor belt. Soon enough a sergeant dragged him away rather unceremoniously, though deservedly. I heard a rumour that he was put on the next 'plane leaving Jeddah – allegedly for Istanbul.

For reasons I do not completely understand, nowhere is the clash of cultures more apparent than between Far Eastern people and Arabs. Western people appear willing to accommodate but Far Easterners seem committed to their own ways. Therefore, the clashes come out in the open with greater clarity than do those between the Arabs and Europeans and Americans.

This story concerns a Korean construction company which won considerable publicity because of the number of contracts they obtained in Saudi Arabia. Competitors and many Saudi officials accused them of using members of the Korean armed forces as labourers. Certainly, Korean workers behave that way. They are glued to their camps, they salute their flag in the morning, line up in military style, and there is an obvious lack of individual life. They have no desire for any contact with the local population. They work longer hours than their Western counterparts, or even labourers from the Indian sub-continent and the Philippines. Their greatest asset is their discipline.

Three years ago, the suspected military or paramilitary organisation of four thousand Korean workers committed to a major project in Eastern Saudi Arabia broke down. There was a strike, there were disturbances, and unknown workers killed their supervisor by crushing him beneath a bulldozer.

Saudi Arabia is no different from any other dictatorship, though it assumes its powers under the mantle of the world's most absolute feudal monarchy. In Saudi Arabia any disturbance, anything out of the ordinary, assumes a greater importance than it deserves, and this was seen as a prelude to more labour disturbances. Considering the presence of a million and a half foreign workers, the incident frightened the government. Justice had to be done, if in a horrifically Saudi way.

The Saudi police gathered the population of the camp at 7.00 one morning, in the area used for daily exercises. They ringed the place with six hundred policemen armed with light and heavy machine guns. There was no need for this show of force. The incident had fizzled out and there were better ways of pursuing the guilty, but this was impossible to explain to the government of the Eastern Region of Saudi Arabia. A major of the Saudi Security Forces marched up and down the lines of Korean workers, pointed to three at random, and asked them to stay behind. The rest were dismissed and returned to their quarters.

The three workers were put on a police truck, driven a few miles from the camp and executed summarily by a Saudi firing squad. Not a single question was asked about their guilt or innocence. Not only were they not questioned, their superiors were not queried. The Koreans put Saudi cash ahead of national pride and never protested – not knowing that the Saudis despised them for not demonstrating more loyalty to their employees.

Weeks later, I had dinner with a Saudi prince who lived in Al Khobar in the Eastern Region and who was a Colonel in the Saudi Air Force. The news of the executions had spread like wildfire and caused much silent, disapproving headshaking. The Prince himself broached the subject and asked me, against my wish, to comment on the rightness or wrongness of Saudi justice. I couldn't help myself; I expressed my doubts. The probable innocence of the three executed men nagged me. I said this as neatly and gently as possible, but was determined to make my point. The Prince's viewpoint was different. According to him, guilt or innocence was immaterial, what mattered was to avoid future incidents by making an example of the three workers. To him, neither Korean workers nor any other workers in the world would dare contemplate disturbing the peace of Saudi Arabia any more. And why should I object when the Koreans didn't?

It is a huge intellectual exercise for someone brought up in Western ways to accept the Prince's point of view. However, no similar disturbance has taken place in Saudi Arabia since and it is said that Saudi authorities tell the story to new arrivals to frighten them into behaving. Under no circumstances can I condone such arbitrary application of 'justice' but the Prince's point was clear; and in a dictatorship the end justifies the means, and the executions worked.

*   *   *

The culture gap leads to lack of faith. People who differ so widely find it hard to trust each other. I was once asked to induce a major American contracting company to re-enter Iraq. This was a highly reputable company, with immense capabilities; it had withdrawn from Iraq at the time of the overthrow of the monarchy in 1958 and not returned. Also, they claimed the Iraqis owed them $3,000,000 which they wanted paid.

The Iraqi Minister of Planning had contacted my associate and through him requested me to go the headquarters of this company in the Mid-West and invite them back to Iraq. My brief included an authorisation to offer the $3,000,000 owed and invite them to negotiate a major railway building contract. A bureaucrat at the Ministry of Planning had discovered that the company had greater expertise in the field than any other in the West, having done some railway building work during the Second World War.

I don't know how appealing the Mid-Western States are in summer or spring or fall. This was February, and extremely cold. I had no choice. I arrived, having telexed the head of the International Division for an appointment. Like a typical travelling salesman, I placed myself at the mercy of the local Holiday Inn. I met the gentleman I came to see first thing the following morning, presented myself as a semi-official emissary of the Iraqi Ministry of Planning and told him of my mission. The prospect of getting $3,000,000 pleased him but he wanted the Iraqis to pay interest; he considered it an overdue loan.

For six days I shuttled back and forth to the largest building in town for meetings with members of management. I was burdened with questions I often could not answer and had to transmit them to London where they were coded and sent to Baghdad. The answers came back the same way. Delaying tactics were being used. The deeper we got into their prospects in Iraq the more technical the questions became, creating a communications log jam. Slowly it became clear that the company was avoiding giving an answer. The one thing common to all officials I met was a desire to prolong my stay in the States. There was something curious in this which eluded me.

I did spend another weekend there and was willing to stay longer if I had an assurance of a 'yes' or 'no'.

I was dealing with one of the world's largest construction companies, which had operated worldwide for many years. International intrigue and entanglements were not new to them. At the end of eight days and nights spent in Joe's Bar, the Melody Lounge and executive suites, their hand was exposed. A telex from London told of a representative of theirs walking into the Ministry of Planning in Baghdad and asking for verification of my credentials.

They did this while I was talking to them. They were not fully convinced of my capability to do what I was promising. Yes, they were worried about the $3,000,000, but the major source of doubt was the Iraqi Government using non-officials to invite them back and to discuss a major contract.

So, there we were. The Iraqi's delegate was in the Mid-West and the company's delegate was in Baghdad. Their representatives met with the Deputy Minister of Planning and pointedly enquired whether I was authorised to negotiate as I had been negotiating. The Deputy's answer was clear. 'Yes, he is . . . sir. We are under the impression that the confidentiality of the matter was impressed upon you by our man. This mission and its contents were to be kept secret.' The representative admitted indiscretion but insisted such matters were too important to them and had to be verified.

Once again, a representative of a major company ran out of the country and I myself hurriedly left the Mid-West. However, contact was re-established with the company; they eventually went into Iraq and tendered for a certain number of projects without my complicating influence. Furthermore, the arrival of the man in Baghdad and his questions about me were accepted not as deviousness on the part of the company but as lack of care on my part. My standing with the Minister of Planning took a long time to recover.

Another bit of Americana involved the president of an oil and gas company. Big as this company was it had never had any dealings with the Middle East and everything they had heard was rather uncomplimentary. While they were not a major international concern they did market liquid propane gas (LPG) and wished to buy some from Saudi Arabia on the open market.

I went to Saudi Arabia to investigate the possibility. My associate there, a powerful businessman, had sold Saudi LPG on the open market. The contact with this American company had considerable appeal. The Saudi government had decided, as a matter of policy, that they wished to deal with independent oil companies to diversify their list of purchasers.

A number of letters and telexes were exchanged with this company before I left London and I had assured its unbelieving president in Texas of the existence and availability of LPG and that he should prepare himself to obtain a visa and journey to Saudi Arabia to join me there. I had not realised just how unbelieving he was; he had heard too many stories about people being involved in a daisy chain and never reaching decision makers or anyone who could influence decision makers.

I spoke to my office in London in code and asked them to telex the doubting Texan to come to Saudi Arabia. A visa was waiting for him at the US Consulate in Houston, Texas. My indirect message told him where I was staying in Jeddah.

To my horror, I received a one-paragraph telex saying: 'Delighted things are progressing but in view of the many misleads to which we have been subjected, I will only come to Saudi Arabia on the invitiation of King Khalid himself. Please get in touch with him and tell him his personal invitation is a requirement for my company to deal with his country. Regards.' He signed his name.

Everyone at the hotel knew of the telex, or so I thought. Everyone, from bellboy to important guests, would have seen this crude reference to Mr Big, he who must never be named in business deals. Astonishingly, and mercifully, this incredible error of judgement, this rare piece of stupidity, did not reach the authorities in Saudi Arabia and I didn't even have to tell my associate about it. I just cut short my journey, came back to London, telephoned the man in Houston and, using the best American I could manage, called him every name in the book. Even after I hung up I don't think the man understood what really happened.

Some misunderstandings are more innocent than others. One of the strangest ones I ever encountered was when I was asked to consult an American company with a problem. The telephone call to arrange a meeting came from the president. As they were one of the top five construction companies in the States I considered the meeting an important one, secretly believing our reputation to have grown greater than it had.

The gentleman, whose company is headquartered in Pittsburgh, appeared in my office accompanied by two of his senior vice-presidents. After the usual exchange of pleasantries I asked if there was anything we might be able to do for them.

The story was simple: three years previously, this company had signed a joint venture agreement with a Saudi partner. No business had been transacted by the joint venture nor were there any prospects of any business. Surely, we agreed, a company of their size and expertise should have won some contracts or be very well on the way to winning some. Something puzzling was happening. It appeared that their Saudi joint venture partner wanted to use them solely as a front.

In this case, the Saudi partner had two other similar arrangements; one with a British, one with a French company. Every time there was a major project the Saudi partner tendered in the names of all three. His offer on behalf of the US company was large, to make his other offers look good. The expense of putting together a tender document and making an offer to meet government specifications on a major construction project is extremely high. Painfully aware of this, the Americans had ceased to acquiesce to our friends' requests and were no longer tendering on anything recommended by him.

This was half of the problem. The other half was their continued interest in Saudi Arabia and desire to work there. After all, a company of their standing was missing out on the world's leading construction market.

This was what the president of this celebrated company came to see me about – their innocent mistake in not investigating their partners thoroughly, and lack of understanding of Arab manipulative skills. He wanted me to help him dissolve his partnership with the Saudi company. If only because Saudi law is written to protect Saudi nationals against outside companies, this would have been very difficult. This banditry was compounded by the fact that the partners were one of the largest trading groups in Saudi Arabia.

For me to lock horns with them would have been dangerous. The money he was offering wouldn't justify the risk.

I could only tell these nice people that I was unable to accept an assignment on their behalf. I explained the difficulties. However, just before the three courteous gentlemen, who clearly needed help, left my office, I decided to give them the benefit of an idea. I suggested they should seek a way out by having the Saudis settle the matter internally without the company appearing to have had anything to do with it.

Specifically, I suggested they work towards becoming close to an influential member of the Saudi Royal Family. To avoid going from the fryingpan into the fire I emphasised the need to be careful about who it was – a prince/businessman they could live with and who could produce work for them. When a relationship had been established, the company's representative could tell the prince of their anxieties over a previous commitment which precluded them from working with him. The finale should be, 'Well, if Your Highness would represent us and petition our agent to release us we would be very happy to work with you, but we do not think that they will break the contract.'

They left appearing to half-accept this idea. Fourteen months later I was very pleased to receive a letter from Pittsburgh, Pennsylvania containing a thank-you note and a cheque for $3,000. My advice had worked. They now have a partner who is very conscientious about their interests and they have managed to win a number of major construction projects in Saudi Arabia.

The persistence with which some people refuse to understand the rather elaborate and sensitive system of communications within the intermediary and skimmer community is a constant source of wonder and fear. Surely, some people just shouldn't deal with the Middle East. Even for those companies who do not wish to use intermediaries it is far better to have someone who understands the system and can say no the right way.

I remember dealing with a former major of the British Army with regard to selling some grenades in the United Arab Emirates. This gentleman had served in the Emirates before their independence and considered himself an expert on the whole area. One thing is certain, he knew all of the names which mattered and he seemed to have dined and wined with all of them over the years.

Our attempts at getting him to co-operate with us and pay us a commission were a failure. He knew the armed forces of the Emirates needed the grenades and so did we. He saw no reason to pay us anything, even when we made it clear we would stop the deal from going through.

The Major was going to the UAE and I hurriedly sent one of my calling cards by courier to the Chief of Procurement of the UAE armed forces – the Colonel to whom we were supposed to sell the grenades, and my associate in the deal. The ex-Major went to see the Chief of Procurement, and while they were discussing the details of the contract the Chief kept flashing my card in the Major's face hoping the signal would be understood. Quite the opposite; the Major's reaction was to tell him, 'I know the man. He's a phony. He kept trying to interfere and get me to pay him a commission.' The Colonel was flabbergasted – the Major missed the point altogether. He didn't even bother to ask why he had the card.

My next instructions were to follow one of the procedures I call dirty tricks. I was asked by the UAE to determine whether the company had any 'Jewish connections', which was easy to do and proved positive. After his return the Major received a letter, not to confirm the order but to inform him that the two Jewish members of his board of directors were known to be contributors to funds for Israel and that his company would not be awarded the contract. Here, the Colonel acted on his own because we opted out of the deal. Instead, the contract went to a co-operative Belgian company.

The differences in cultural values certainly include a difference in attitudes to money. Not only does the Koran command Moslems to speak of it, those who have it are impelled to flaunt it. Now that some of them have it in huge quantities their sense of it is completely different from the others'. As a matter of fact, the abuse of money has reached a scale unknown in recorded history.

One of my associates in Saudi Arabia happens to be the largest private owner of tankers in the whole Middle East. He owns sixteen of them including three 350,000 tonners.

This is an impressive fleet of ships by any international standards and because of hazards such as the quality of education of the crews and bunkering people, plus the inherent political instability of the Middle East, the insurance rates on these ships are extremely high. When I last looked at the insurance policies, he was paying something of the magnitude of $560,000 a month.

These insurance policies were being placed through a Greek agent in Athens who was not an insurance expert but knew a little about shipping and tankers. Since he had helped my friend purchase two of his tankers, he was allowed to handle everything relating to them.

As I was connected with a major insurance company in New York, I asked them about their possible interest in the business. They were interested, and wanted to examine the policies and the history of damages and claims. When I went back to my friend to solicit his insurance business, he said he was very willing for me and the New York company to present him with a new insurance programme but he wasn't willing to expend any effort in showing us the history of damages and claims and the most he could do was give us copies of the insurance policies.

After much contemplation of the prospects, we accepted this limited information as a base upon which we could present him with a new insurance programme. A representative travelled to Saudi Arabia and received these instructions from my associate: 'I am interested in your insurance programme if it saves me money, but it has to be worthwhile money.' Two months later the same representative and myself went to Jeddah with a policy identical to the one originating with the Greek but 18% cheaper. We were able to save him so much money because his Athens insurance man had been dishonest: he had not passed on any discounts or rebates to the Saudi tycoon.

We had a meeting with our Saudi businessman and explained how we could save him well over a million dollars a year. Incredible as it sounds, he looked at us and said, 'How much did you say, over a million dollars? I can't change to you for one million dollars a year – it isn't worth it to me. After all, Johnny the Greek is my friend. If you guys had told me that was all it was going to be I would have saved you the time and effort.'

We found ourselves utterly speechless. We had never known anyone who didn't respect a million dollars. We closed the meeting awkwardly.

The following morning, having decided that the man's mind was set against our plan, we petitioned his managing director to reimburse us for our out-of-pocket expenses, which amounted to $24,000. The managing director did make the request on our behalf. We were turned down completely.

When it comes to money, the Arab is both a spender and full of pettiness. We considered it would have been fair and right for him to pay our expenses. After all, by any yardstick a saving of over a million dollars a year is worthwhile. To him a million dollars was not worth the friendship of his old associate. Yet he was not prepared to reimburse us for our efforts, though the sum was much smaller.

There is, of course, the problem of time. The Arab does not believe in fact but in meaning, so for him keeping time is part of an impossible syndrome: the belief in everything being in the hands of Allah. This is, of course, extremely difficult today when you have to meet 'plane schedules and when, more often than not, you have other people you want to see.

Not only does the Arab not believe in time, his prelude to a business conversation seems to be agonisingly long, particularly to the average businessman who is not accustomed to Middle Eastern ways. There are the questions about one's health, one's kids, one's family in general and all kinds of other details that are not pertinent to the subject under consideration. Also, we're not talking about people who are checking on the welfare of a family they know, they do it strictly out of habit. Very often an Arab businessman will ask a Western visitor how his kids are, only to be startled by their non-existence.

The Western precept, 'a time and a place for everything', implying among other things that a business meeting is for the discussion of business, means nothing to most Arabs. One of the most successful intermediaries I know has problems with women. He falls in love regularly and painfully, and moans unashamedly when his women leave.

Among my friend's all-time favourites was a British Airways stewardess who, after a few weeks of fun and expensive presents, wanted no more of him. His pleadings fell on deaf ears and he behaved ridiculously, even hiring a detective agency to chase the poor girl around.

The Dutch representatives of a major arms company and I were visiting my intermediary friend when he received a telephone call from his private detective. We were sitting in the bar of the London Hilton, a busy room full of rude waiters and heavy leather furniture. My friend took the call outside.

Soon he returned, looking very pale. 'He is a black man, a black man,' he said. On enquiry, 'he' turned out to be the stewardess's new boyfriend.

We wanted to talk business, but our sick friend kept muttering, 'Nigger, God damn it.' The Dutchman couldn't take it any more. He said the problem was imminently soluble, and gave my friend a detailed description of the advantages of black Kiwi shoe polish.

My intermediary friend left the bar huffily and I haven't seen him since. May all his days be white.

My last story in the area of cultural clashes has to do with one of the more subtle aspects of understanding the Middle East; some appreciation of the attitudes of the Moslem religion.

I was trying to set up an insurance company in the Eastern part of Saudi Arabia for the owner of a local truck-leasing company. This man owned over two thousand trucks which he leased to Aramco and to construction companies. He was very prosperous. On paper, it looked like a perfect situation for the creation of an insurance company to save him money by covering his in-house business and perhaps, if he thought it advisable, he could handle business on the outside. The savings to him out of a programme like that were in excess of half a million dollars a year.

I gathered all the necessary details and discussed them with an American group who specialised in creating 'captive' insurance companies. We drew up a plan and a representative and I went to Eastern Saudi Arabia to meet the trucker.

Being an intuitive Bedouin, he had absolutely no problem in understanding the plan. He was willing to sign the agreement, was very thankful to us and pleased to pay my commission and whatever fee was required by the American company.

The trouble started over dinner. The man was so pleased with the deal that he was treating us to a meal in the grand Arab style. There were seven of us around a table in a local Lebanese restaurant in the middle of which was a whole roasted lamb. The host proceeded to tear away huge chunks of lamb and place them on the plate of his American guest who was supposed to eat them. He certainly wasn't supposed to say no, regardless of the state of his appetite. Well, this process isn't an easy one and all kinds of grease and fat and rice and other bits ended up on my American friend's suit. I could see from a distance that he didn't appreciate it but this was to be a minor problem.

The major problem started when we moved from discussing amiable nothings to discussing business. My American friend, not knowing how Moslems feel about money and insurance, advised his host to enter the life insurance field. He added, with a big smile, 'That's where the money is, and if you tell me all of those people out there are uninsured they should do something about it. After all they should leave something for their families after they die.' This was a violation of everything the Saudi had learned. It recalled every religious bit in the recesses of his narrow mind and it offended him beyond words.

To a Moslem, life is in the hands of God. You do not insure against death because only the Creator decides when and how. The Saudi Government is against life insurance. To our Saudi associate, the Koran is against life insurance. For someone to suggest at his table that this should be otherwise was indeed heresy.

My wink signals finally got through to my American friend and he stopped the conversation. Everything else stopped too. The following morning, the Saudi telephoned me and told me he did not wish to deal with us. We had insulted Islam and should leave Saudi Arabia right away. I uselessly pleaded but we left Saudi Arabia without the deal we had already completed, the captive company.

My experiences of business problems arising out of cultural differences are shared by many. Unfortunately, they repeat themselves every day. The Westernisation of the Middle East is waist high. The area's mind and soul belong to a different world.

7

How to Capture a Company

If an intermediary cannot obtain the co-operation of companies to work with him, he is a failure. True, there are more companies than there are sheikhs and emirs, so that having the right sheikh or emir remains the effective intermediary's most important asset. But the particular talent to 'capture' a company comes a close second. Also, an intermediary wins an emir or a sheikh once, then works hard to maintain the relationship. In the case of companies he is negotiating with new ones constantly and his ability to 'seduce' them is always on trial.

You start to win when you get through to 'authorised' representatives. About a third of all solicitations die before such a contact takes place. Sometimes this failure is due simply to circumstances – for example, a company may have previous commitments in the intermediary's country of interest. Sometimes failure occurs because the telephone contact or opening letter is not enticing enough for the company to continue discussions. The impression created by the first contact is extremely important, since companies are subjected to innumerable solicitations of every type. An intermediary must try to give his approach individual character, to avoid having it smack of déjà vu.

Mystery and appeal should feature in the initial approach. A telephone contact is preferable, except when the intermediary doesn't consider the instrument safe. It's more human and engaging, and gives one more opportunity to convince the company a meeting should take place and more flexibility in fixing one up.

Some desired meetings with corporations never materialise

because contact is made at the wrong level. An 'authorised' representative is a senior management one. Many intermediaries make the mistake of going to the man in charge of the Middle East, or the export director. Since these are the very people whose lack of expertise often necessitates the use of an intermediary, it is no wonder if their attitude to approaches is negative. And I have already mentioned that export directors, etc., are frequently jealous of the amount of money intermediaries can make. One is always better off going to the very top of the company where there are no personal jealousies and the only interest is in doing business. The dented ego of the export director can be attended to later. So, make your pitch, your sales message, distinct from others', and reach someone at the top.

The company should never be told all the facts available to the intermediary before signing an agreement. Always hold back on some of these facts or pretend you are holding back. Companies are much more intrigued by what they don't know than by what they know. In addition, the nature of the business makes them attach considerable importance to what they don't know – they feel they are missing out on the make-or-break factor. Besides, why give them all the facts and have them turn around and act without you?

Intermediaries must be flexible. The nature of their business does not allow them to be rigid and they seldom are. However, some appear to lack dexterity in presenting their financial demands, which is very frightening to the corporation. Always use small numbers, the percentage figure rather than the money figure. Let's face it, in policy matters it is much easier for an intermediary to change his ways of doing business than it is for a corporation, whatever its size.

An intermediary must be mentally equipped with more than one formula to realise the amount of money he and his group want. This is always pleasing to the company. It avoids the unnecessary complications of being hemmed in by one formula, which may be illegal or against company or national policy, and speeds up the corporate decision-making process.

Another sweetener is the history-of-success spiel, which helps corporations feel secure with a particular intermediary. A good intermediary should always refer to success stories by the name of the project and not by the name of the company with which he worked. This gives a false aura of protecting the confidence of others and is reassuring to his prospective client.

In purely practical terms, an intermediary should have references for himself and his master. It is highly advisable to have friends in recognised business corporations and banking circles who would always vouch for you; not necessarily your own bankers. One's own bankers tend to be officious and, in the case of successful intermediaries, secretive and out of the country. Therefore they are not a good source. But other respectable members of the banking community can be tremendously helpful. The good word of a member of the management of a leading international corporation represents a neutral judgement and can be a great help.

I have, over the years, had the good fortune to know people who would willingly testify on my behalf without having done business with me. They represent leading US and German banks, a number of British and US international corporations, as well as well-known international lawyers.

I should like to tell a story to illustrate the various obstacles to be overcome when meeting a corporation for the first time. I managed, through some personal contacts, to reach a member of the board of Tarmac Construction, one of the major construction companies in the UK, and arranged to meet him at 10.00 one morning. When I was ushered into his office the gentleman was on the 'phone, so I sat down and waited while he continued talking about some project in Nigeria.

When he finished, he put the receiver back, sat down and without saying welcome or shaking my hand looked up and said, 'Aburish, are you a sheikh?' 'No, sir, I am not, I am an ordinary man.' 'Good,' came the retort. 'I have sheikhs coming out of my ears. Now, sir, what can I do for you?'

For two hours I attempted to overcome the man's natural resistance to the use of intermediaries by a recitation of projects completed, who our associates were and the type of decent, businesslike folks we ourselves were. At first he would not be moved, and kept interrupting my organised oral presentation with side questions like, 'Why the hell are the Iraqis building so many bathrooms in their railway stations – those guys don't use bathrooms in the first place.'

Our meeting continued over lunch, where I got the distinct impression he was trying to get me to open up by getting me drunk. As I am not by nature a lunchtime drinker he had little success in this department but continued needling, teasing, abrasively questioning. He had seen intermediaries before. He was a likeable man of about sixty who had obviously come up the hard way and was using his intrinsic good sense and knowledge of humanity to find 'the facts'.

Nothing had been concluded when we parted company, though I had done my best. By the time I reached my office, which was considerably further from the restaurant than his, telephone messages awaited me from two banker friends. I rang back to find that my lunch host had asked them about my bona fides. My ploy to drop their names into the conversation had worked marvellously; he did contact them and they gave me good recommendations.

In the end Tarmac agreed to work with us. They agreed because we managed to meet them in person, satisfied them that we were well connected, were businesslike, had a considerable list of successes to our name and had useful sheikhs or emirs or others behind us. Besides, we had the right references and proved to be agile and flexible and able to take the superficial abuses of their man for half a day. This is what it takes to entice a corporation to work with your team. Package yourself to look like no other. It is impossible to predict that first encounter, but one should be prepared as far as possible. After all, selling intangibles is the most difficult thing in the world.

8

Money – Where It Goes

Exact figures for Arab oil income are not available. This is due to the multiplicity of deals and prices, bartering, producing over OPEC-designated quotas, and giving friends favourable price and payment terms. One thing is certain: in spite of the decline in oil consumption we are still dealing with hundreds of billions of dollars annually, enough money to satisfy the Middle East and to make more business for intermediaries and skimmers.

1983 was a vague year for figures because it suffered most from overt oil production activity (producing over OPEC-designated levels and selling at low prices). A more accurate estimate of the Arab countries' oil income is possible for 1982 and it produces a figure near $150,000,000,000. Supposing two-thirds of that, $100,000,000,000, went into intermediary/skimmer commissionable business – with an average commission level of 7% it produced pay-offs worth $7,000,000,000.

Seven billion dollars a year is larger than the budget of Jordan, a country of 4,000,000 people, larger than the budget of Syria, with a population of 11,000,000. It is larger than the US non-military aid programme. Seven billion dollars a year is big money.

Let us take a look at how this figure is contracted for, hidden, spent, or invested. To begin with, most of the money is spent in unbelievably wasteful, vulgar ways. The stories are endless but some bear repeating.

Gambling is one way to squander money and the Arabs gamble in Monaco, London, Las Vegas, wherever. A close friend of King Hussein of Jordan, a former Ford Motor Company agent, dropped

£4,000,000 in a London casino in one evening. He tried to avoid paying some of it, the casino wrote to the King and the debt was met. Saudi Arabia's Sheikh Yamani reputedly had his own room at London's Playboy Club. He played against the wheel all by his lonesome.

In 1974 Prince Fahd of Saudi Arabia (before becoming King) lost $6,000,000 gambling in Monte Carlo in one evening and nearly lost his number three place in the line of succession to the throne. When summoned by King Faisal to explain his misdeeds he insisted it was another Fahd (it's a common family name) and not him. Faisal, not a wordly man, accepted the explanation.

Money is also squandered in flamboyant gestures. Naim Kaalagy, a Jordanian intermediary, bought four hundred Hermes ties to take back to Amman as presents for friends. A UAE businessman offered an English beauty £500,000 to go to bed with him. To his amazement she refused so he bought her a sports Mercedes as a measure of his affection. She took the car and didn't return the affection. A Saudi businessman bought three identical copies of a diamond necklace at half a million dollars a piece. They were presented with considerable flourish during one week to three willing recipients. There is reason to believe the ladies liked the necklaces.

All of the waste aside, there is still money left to save and invest. Commission money is received in accordance with agreements stipulating method and place of payment. Most of them speak of payment to a 'bank in a place of your choice' (the intermediary's), and most of them stipulate pro rata payments, payments to the intermediary as payments are received by the company from the government.

When the agreement is made by a large corporation for large sums of money, considerable care is taken to safeguard its contents and only a single copy is made. This copy is deposited in a bank for safekeeping, can be seen by either the company's representatives or the intermediary but cannot be withdrawn except by both. Oerlikon, the major Swiss arms maker, contracted with Dr Ruth Fahmy, among other things, to sell an aerial defence system costing $1.2 billion to Iraq. They wrote to Dr Fahmy, telling her that the document concerning remuneration had been placed in a bank, but such was their concern for secrecy that they did not mention the bank by name.

Companies are happy to abide by these methods, but they have a natural reluctance to pay either in the country where they are registered or the country where the project takes place. They want to place it as far away from them as possible.

The details of where and how money is paid are determined by the size of the deal. A single, very large transaction deserves the setting up of a corporation whose sole purpose is to handle this transaction. After the deal is done, and all monies have been received, they are transferred to places unknown and the corporation is dissolved. Liechtenstein, Switzerland, the Channel Islands, the Dutch West Indies and other territories with no income tax obligations, are the natural grounds for a one-shot big deal corporation.

Smaller deals are handled less elaborately. The monies can be deposited in a bank anywhere. Again, care must be taken to avoid taxation, otherwise no complicated organisation is needed.

When more than one person is involved in a deal and there is an apparent lack of trust, more complicated instructions are required. I was once party to a deal where the company didn't want to enter more than one payment in its books and my associate and I didn't trust each other. The solution was to open a joint bank account which neither could touch without the other's permission to accommodate our joint efforts.

After a deal is done, spending sprees aside, money (particularly when the sums are large) must find a home. Arabs on the whole prefer to invest in things they can see and feel, like real estate. Several of London's leading hotels, including the Park Tower and Kensington Palace, are owned by Arabs. So is the legendary Ritz in Paris. Saudi businessman Gaith Pharoan bought a big chunk of downtown Atlanta. His brother Mazen owns thousands of acres of land around Santa Barbara, California. The former head of National Security in Saudi Arabia, Kamal Adham, finds small business jets suffocating and uses a long-distance Boeing 727.

After real estate, Arabs like to invest in corporations. Saudi businessman Sulaiman Olayan controls Whittaker Corporation, one of the leading hospital management and medical care companies in the world. The Kuwaitis' investment fund bought 20%

of Mercedes Benz. Saudi intermediary Akram Oje of Tag Corporation sells Falcon corporate jets, Sheikh Zayed of Abu Dhabi indirectly controls the Bank of Credit and Commerce and at the last count sixty new banks were incorporated in seven years.

The intangible entity, a service business, does not have the same appeal as either 'concrete' or money handling. However, there are instances of money going into self-aggrandisement schemes. UAE's Ambassador to the UK, Mahdi Al Tajer, brought out an English-language magazine called *Eight Days*. It failed, costing him millions of dollars. On the other hand, Prince Sulman of Saudi Arabia controls a Saudi publishing house which produces well-edited dailies and weeklies loyal to the House of Saud.

There are conservative types who don't believe in investing at all. They keep their money in bank deposits or gold. The recent fluctuation in the price of gold, and bank crises in the UK, have put their old-fashioned ways to the test. They are looking for bigger, safer storehouses, which is proving difficult. A Saudi businessman told me with pride how he moved his money from Citibank to Morgan Guarantee. It was funny listening to him; the guttural r's in Morgan Guarantee would have offended the lily-white founding fathers.

At the end of the day few people have invested their money wisely. The number of rags to riches back to rags stories is legion. Sheikh Farhan Al Tantani made over five million dollars working for Aramco, lost it on wine, women and song, made another ten and lost it and made yet another ten to lose it with no chance of recovery. He is an engaging little man who looks like a darker version of Lenin. Unrepentant, he still sees nothing wrong with using $100 notes like calling cards.

Increased competition has placed pressure on the level of commissions. There are fewer intermediaries and money isn't as free and easy as in the heady days of the 1970s. But the survivors are big-timers dealing with big money. They have changed with the times, invested and saved and, like the Mafia, moved into legitimate business.

9

---❧❧❧---

Dirty Tricks at High Noon

It should be clear by now that I have no moral problem in tolerating the intermediary establishment, but see it as a traditional institution aimed at distributing wealth. I do object to the excesses, to the way this facet of Arab culture has been abused. It is the excesses, with their implications of corruption and intrigue, which have caught the headlines and prevented a better understanding of the institution, its history and what oil wealth has done to it.

One of the more objectionable aspects of today's intermediary business is the department of dirty tricks; what people do to undermine competitors, promote or trick associates, violate laws and commit crimes to win a piece of business, to make money. I am delighted to report that my own firm has never knowingly been involved in any such questionable efforts, in spite of being on the receiving end a good number of times.

Tapping competitors' telephones is commonplace, boring. This doesn't stop it from being an effective means of gathering information and demoralising the competition. Believing one's telephone to be tapped makes one uneasy, suspicious, fearful. The victim's awareness of it may stop him from compromising himself, but it doesn't lessen the doubt and discomfort. This means that the perpetrators succeed even if they fail – i.e. are discovered.

During 1975–76, I was working for my Iraqi associates on a deal involving armaments – an area of interest to fellow intermediaries and to intelligence establishments. Information about Iraq's armament programme was and is important to Israeli, Iranian,

Western and Russian intelligence organisations. It was equally important to other intermediaries. Even companies such as Plessey Electronics, Westland Helicopter and Fabrique Nationale of Belgium were interested as potential suppliers. For any of these parties, inside information would enable them to make the right moves to promote their policies, the companies they represented, or their products. And I discovered my telephone was tapped.

My then secretary was an upper-class English lady who affected a phony lisp and relished high airs. She was a tall, pretty and totally social creature, full of good manners and gossip. Though unaware of most of my activities, she suspected dark things, but liked the job because the pay was good and the work undemanding.

We shared a single large office in an old converted building in Sackville Street, London W1. We were in full view of each other all the time. One day I asked her to make theatre reservations for me. She was trying to dial the theatre when all of a sudden she dropped the receiver and began to scream. I ran over to comfort her and eventually, through gestures, sobs and half-words, I was told the telephone was tapped. I picked up the receiver and listened, to hear a recording of a conversation my secretary had had the day before. I put down the receiver, signalled her to leave the office with me and took her down the street to the local café to discuss the matter.

There was no doubt as to the tapping. But did the culprits make a mistake by pushing the play instead of record button, or were they trying to frighten us? In either case what was I to do? Talking Miss Fancy-Lisp into not resigning proved easier than expected. Strangely, the unexpected excitement appealed to something dormant in her aristocratic make-up. My next move was to call, from a telephone booth, my lawyer, who was full of amusement and common sense.

The first course of action the lawyer and I considered was to go to the police, make an issue out of it and be subjected to questions I didn't want to answer. A second choice would be to mislead whoever it was by feeding them wrong information. Thirdly, one could hire a debugging expert. I opted for the last suggestion.

The debugging expert, sent by my lawyer, entered my office after knocking, ran all the way to the end of the office where I was sitting, put one hand on my mouth and signalled me to keep quiet with the other. He then gently led me outside to find out what had happened. My secretary and I told him the story.

The first thing the debugging expert did was to wander around the place with a mine-detector type of small gadget which was supposed to signal the presence of bugs. He unscrewed the telephone receivers, looked inside desks and closets and examined windows carefully. Nothing was found. Then he began examining telephone wires and suddenly, according to his pointing finger, there it was. An extra wire covered with some type of cream which was dirtied with dust to make it look old.

He traced the wire to the hallway outside the office and then to a conduit which lead to the basement. Without saying a word, I motioned him to cut it, which he did with a pair of special scissors.

That was the end of the story in terms of eliminating the tap. But questions remained and remain to this day. Who did it, and was the landlord involved? Did whoever did it pick up valuable information? Should I have told my Iraqi associates?

I did not tell them, and I never discovered the answers. I started making important telephone calls from outside, moved my important files to a bank safe, had the debugging expert inspect the office every month and gave my secretary an increase in salary to keep her mouth shut. It was a costly response.

A much easier way of determining what the competition is doing is to spy on them in the old-established manner, by buying off one of their employees. To my dismay this is what our associate in Oman did and probably still does, though he lost us because of it.

We had an agreement to represent the company of Sayed Fahr, the Sultan of Oman's uncle and the second most important man in that country. The management of his company was made up of Greek Cypriots and overseas Greeks. Like a lot of aggressive minorities they are not known for their moral scruples. The managing director's talent was questionable, but he was a determined and ambitious young man.

Omani Trading and Industrial Engineering Organisation (OTIEO) required our help to present an offer to equip two schools with everything they needed, the equipment being provided by a British company. These were medium-sized contracts, but bore a high level of commission, as do most equipping jobs. The total contract value was estimated at over $4,000,000.

I was visiting Oman to check on the progress of this project and others, to compensate for the usual lack of communication from the other end. The managing director of His Highness's company reported that our chances of winning the school equipping contract were good. Our main competitor was an Italian company sponsored by one of the leading trading families in the country. The trading family couldn't match Prince Fahr in influence, but it was feared that the Italian suppliers would offer much lower prices than the British company operating under our umbrella.

My simplisitic answer to competitive situations like this is to carry out a thorough examination of the chief rivals and their record of success in the past, in an attempt to beat them in terms of both price and approach to the project. To my associate this meant unnecessary work. As far as he was concerned, the best answer was the direct one of finding out exactly what our competitors were doing, handing the information to our people and asking them to improve upon it.

Accordingly, he had bribed the telex operator at the office of the trading family, who had sold him a copy of the offer made by the Italian group for the miserable sum of £50. As far as I know, my contact was acting on his own initiative, without the knowledge of the head of the organisation.

This presented us with a dilemma. There was no way we could act on this information but, simultaneously, we didn't want to lose OTIEO as an associate. I left Oman not knowing what to do.

On returning to London and reviewing OTIEO's file, I discovered a lot more things which were highly questionable, including a possibility that we had been cheated out of some commissions. I put all this information together and wrote a letter of complaint to the Prince. There was a remote chance he would appreciate our honesty and discipline or fire his henchman.

Our complaint fell upon deaf ears; the Prince stuck by his man and cancelled our contract. Our Greek friend is gone, probably buying competitors' telexes for another master. In fairness, there is no way to determine whether Sayed Fahr was involved or not. It is more likely that he was protecting someone he was fond of.

*   *   *

Intermediaries are not the only people involved in Middle Eastern business deals who resort to underhand practices. The travelling company representative, the man who pays periodic visits to the Middle East, is a complex creature. He resents being the odd man out, living off his modest salary when everyone else is taking cuts of enormous sums. He has a strong desire to be directly involved, financially. His interjecting himself as a part of the pay-off arrangement is dealt with elsewhere in this book, but he sometimes resorts to unorthodox methods.

One of the more unwholesome sources of extra money for company salesmen (and occasionally other export executives) is moonlighting. Selling to the Middle East is expensive. Many companies cannot afford to do it on their own. As a result, some representatives accept the illicit approaches of companies other than their employers to work for them on the side. No one can know how many people they represent when they are in far away Yemen or Bahrain.

This is more prevalent among British salesmen, who are re-latively poorly paid, than with any other national group. I know of an arms saleman who represents a direct competitor of his em-ployer on a commission basis; others have what they describe as 'my own interests', and yet others have long-term contracts with outside companies. The most common moonlighting activity in the arms business is when a member of management deals legally for the company and illegally for himself. If the foreign office refuses a licence to a country to import X products from a reputable British firm, one of the firm's executives may fulfil the order illegally on his own behalf.

Some representatives cheat their own companies in a more direct way. They occasionally set up a decoy intermediary when there is none. This only happens in small deals. The Middle East area sales manager of a British company making educational aids received a follow-up order from Bahrain after having dispensed with their agent/intermediary. He called on a friend of his in Holland, asked him to pretend he was the intermediary on the deal, and the two split up a commission of 10% of the total value of the order (£50,000).

*　　*　　*

The most destructive kind of dirty trick is when an intermediary corners the whole market on a project. In other words, he manages to represent all the companies competing for a single project. This deliberate, elaborate manipulation of companies involves great deceit and often has a discouraging and demoralising effect on its victims. It also reflects poorly on the intermediary fraternity, the intelligence of the companies and overall business in the Middle East.

An operator in the Emirates, we will call him TS, sponsored George Wimpey & Company and Shand Construction of the UK and the German contractor Wyess & Freytag for the same project. Wimpey won the contract but it cost the other two companies £50,000 each to compete. The Ministry of Education in Saudi Arabia issues one huge list of its requirements of sports goods on an annual basis (300,000 footballs, 500,000 jerseys, etc.). In 1983, three companies, one Brazilian, one from Hong Kong, one Korean, placed the first, second and third best offers to fulfil the order. They were represented by the same man.

An uglier variation on this theme is when the company consents to be part of the deception. Intermediaries have talked companies into deliberately making losing offers to point up the winning aspects of a rival offer, in return for a cut of the intermediaries' commission. In fairness to companies, this has resulted from an if-you-can't-beat-them-join-them act of desperation.

The dirtiest tricks to fight are the ones when you can neither complain, sue, nor change things in a beneficial way. A company can give an intermediary a limited duration agreement and refuse to renew it after he gets them well established. The Italian munitions supplier Tirena SA makes flame-throwers and gunpowder. They used our good offices to obtain a small trial order for the UAE. They promised us a new agreement later. Once they knew the business was coming their way, they reneged on the whole deal. There was nothing we could do. Even if we could have taken them to court we wouldn't have wanted to because of the ensuing damage to our 'other activities'.

MEL, a division of Phillips Electronics, authorised my friend Glen Hobday and I to offer their equipment in Saudi Arabia. We did so, using the offices of an influential sheikh. As the prospects were long-term rather than immediate, the sheikh contacted MEL behind our backs. Instead of renewing their agency with us they went with him. Again, there is very little one can do. Making too much noise is counterproductive.

It may be worth my while, however, to make a noise about the conduct of my 'colleague' Dr Ruth Fahmy. Ruth Fahmy is unique – the only female arms dealer in the Middle East. She approached me for help, and we signed an explicit and permanent agreement to co-operate on armaments deals in Iraq, where I have useful contacts (see Chapter 8). The two big projects covered by the agreement are for Oerlikon to sell Iraq defence equipment worth $1.2 billion and for the German contractor Heilit & Woerner to build a $200,000,000 munitions factory.

Ruth was introduced to my friends in Baghdad. They are helping her in her efforts to win those contracts.

In spite of the clarity of our agreement, Ruth refuses to tell me what is happening. My friends keep me informed to some extent, and I haven't told them that Ruth is behaving badly. In this case, the money involved is enough for me to resort to the courts. Ruth and I and my Iraqi friends are likely to be damaged by it all.

A large UK engineering firm used the UAE intermediary TS, acting in association with myself, to make a £20,000,000 offer on a medium girder military bridge. A commission of 7% is payable to TS and myself. News reached me in March 1984 that they had won the contract. When I wrote to enquire, their lawyers replied that they had never heard of me. Well, there is enough correspondence to suggest otherwise. Perhaps another case for my enterprising solicitor.

All of this goes to prove that little honour exists in the business, and what there is falls under the heading of honour among thieves.

10

Death in Baghdad

In the Middle East the building of railways is not accorded the same priority as other, more obvious development projects such as building highways or oil-related concerns like refineries and petro-chemical plants. Nevertheless, some railway projects are just as big as these other schemes, and they are more demanding on expertise. So little railway building has been done anywhere in the world in the last thirty years that few companies have any experience of it.

Iraq is almost twice the size of the UK with a population of 12,000,000 people, relatively evenly dispersed. It is very much in need of a railway system to connect its various regions. This need is accentuated by the diversity of the Iraqi economy. It has the second highest proven oil reserves in the Middle East after Saudi Arabia; the Tigris and Euphrates rivers give it immense agro-industrial and hydro-electrical potential; and it contains iron-ore deposits in the North and supposedly the world's largest phosphate mines located in the West, in the corner bordering Jordan and Syria.

Iraq, rightly, is less dependent on oil than are other Middle Eastern countries. As a result, Iraqi planners are committed to developing their other natural resources, including the phosphate deposits. A massive contract to mine the desert expanse rich in phosphates was awarded to a Belgian consortium headed by a company called Sybatra. This development is taking place in several stages over a period of fifteen years, with the first phase costing $1,700,000,000. This began in 1976 and ended in 1982.

Immediately following the mine development award to Sybatra, the Iraqis addressed themselves to the inevitable problem of transporting that phosphate from Akashat, the only town in the otherwise desolate area, to Baghdad and then south to the port of Basra, to be shipped throughout the world. There already was a railway link between Baghdad and Basra – but none between Akashat and Baghdad.

The distance between Akashat and Baghdad is four hundred and ninety kilometres of barren, brutal land where nothing grows. It is demanding in engineering terms because the soil characteristics change from fine shifting sand to dry crumbly limestone. Both cause problems for the building and maintaining of railways. Aside from parts of the US and Australia, terrain like this has never been negotiated by railway builders.

The Iraqi decision to make a feasibility study of this project was taken with alacrity. The study part was carried out by a subsidiary of British Rail. Invitations were prepared for companies to tender for its actual construction (laying of the track and the building of the various stations along the way). While the total cost of such a project is never known until a final contract is awarded, it was established at about $2,500,000,000.

It was and perhaps remains the largest single contract of its type in the history of the Middle East. The financial requirements placed it beyond the means of most construction companies to undertake alone and few of them, particularly in the West, had the expertise. Except for minor, troublesome efforts in Africa and South America, people had been dismantling rather than building railroads.

Our Iraqi promoter on this project was the late Adnan Hamdani, then Minister of Planning and Deputy Prime Minister of the Republic of Iraq, member of the Supreme Command of the ruling Baath Party and indisputedly the second most important man in the land. Hamdani contacted my associate in Baghdad and informed him that within six days invitations were going to major construction companies to tender for this contract. The invitees were a select number of companies, about five. Companies who were aware of the project were already lobbying to get themselves on the list of invitees. Some had hounded members of the Ministry of Planning with expressions of interest and flooded them with masses of literature about their qualifications.

Hamdani wanted a British company or consortium to tender for the project for political reasons. Iraq–UK relations, previously fragile, were on the mend. My associate and I were to make the 'business arrangement' as soon as possible before the official invitations went out. In view of the size of the project, the amounts of money being asked in commission and the time scale this was almost an impossible request. While Hamdani had no particular British company in mind, he favoured a well-known international constructor whom we will call DIB*. DIB's reputation and size appealed to him and his associates. The US's construction giant Morrison Knudsen, with more recent railway building experience in the West, had declined to be considered because of deep involvement in the Alaska Pipeline.

A special messenger from my associate flew from Baghdad to London to brief me on the details and the mechanics of tendering. By the time he arrived and I had digested all the available information, I had a total of four days left during which to effect an agreement calling for a British company to pay Mr Hamdani and his group no less than 4% on the value of the contract. In addition I needed a separate agreement for my company of ½%, making a total of $112,500,000 commission.

I had no substitute for DIB – just in case one was needed. I didn't know anyone within the DIB organisation. The immediate question was who at DIB to ask for US $112,500,000 in commissions and how to finalise all of this – in writing – within the given time.

I called DIB on the blind, having obtained the telephone number of their corporate headquarters from the directory. I asked for the man in charge of their Middle Eastern operations. I talked myself past his secretary to the man himself. I told him I had something too important to discuss on the telephone and that I must meet him to discuss it in person as soon as possible. Besides this mysterious promise, I shared with him the secret about DIB being banned in Iraq because of its close relations with the previous regime and implied an ability to discuss the lifting of this ban. I knew they wanted to re-enter Iraq.

---

* DIB is an invented acronym, taken from the chapter title.

We met the following morning on neutral territory, in a small café in Chelsea. He identified me by my guise of a blue suit and red tie. He was red-headed and had an RAF-style bushy moustache. We sat in a small, secluded corner where I introduced myself in hushed tones and gave him a card with my home address and telephone number already written on it. Without preliminaries, I told him I wanted to discuss the largest single construction project in the history of Iraq and DIB's possible interest in it.

My approach, of necessity, was very direct. I had no time to lose. I told him about the project, the invitations and the time scale. The Iraqis, I maintained, would stay with the original list of invitees under all circumstances. I told him of DIB's favourable position in spite of their recent history of inactivity in Iraq. Their continued presence on the list of invitees depended on their willingness to give us two agreements. These were to be written with Iraqi anti-intermediary laws 8 and 52 in mind – the laws which prohibit intermediary activity. The major agreement for 4% was earmarked for Hamdani and an agreement for ½% was for my group. In return, I promised that hours after these agreements were signed, a telex invitation to DIB to tender for this contract would arrive in their offices addressed to him in person. The ban on the company would eventually be lifted and a company representative would be invited to fly to Iraq to see Mr Hamdani and others.

There was some discussion about their ability to undertake a contract of this size and the need for a number of sub-contractors. There was more discussion about verifying our assurance to take them off the Iraqis' blacklist and there was obvious worry about the feasibility of all of this considering the time limit. However, DIB was eager for work and the man was unimpressed by the list of would-be competitors, believing the only people capable of causing DIB any trouble were the Indians, who operated and maintained the second largest railway system in the free world and whose labour is cheap. All of this took an hour. We agreed to meet again the next day.

At 11.00 a.m. the following day we met at their offices in west London. My contact was accompanied by two men, both of whom had had experience in the Middle East. The points discussed the previous day were discussed again, expanded upon, examined with care, but still there was no decision. The problem was the sub-contractors and the time scale, not my ability to convince them. They accepted the combination of the telex being addressed to the man by name and including certain wordings referring to the previous entanglement which got them blacklisted as proof of my representing the 'right people'. They believed in my relationship with Hamdani no matter how indirect.

Our meeting continued over a sandwich lunch but nothing new was said. I was beginning to wonder whether there was any particular reason for the meeting and was very close to voicing this doubt when one of them pointed to his watch and declared that it was 2.30 p.m., time to see the Vice-Chairman. The Vice-Chairman, a portly man in his mid-fifties, with an air of traditional British imperturbability, was waiting for us and went through various gestures of hospitality, including seating me on his right and ordering coffee.

The verbal exchanges of the past two meetings were replayed in an abbreviated version. I assured the man of the Iraqi Government's basic desire to have DIB back in Iraq – of their conditional wish to have them win this project. However, unless we moved fast and secured this invitation, getting DIB back into Iraq would take several months and they would be too late to compete for this job. In answer to his only question of why them, I stated Iraq's political reasons for wishing to give the project to a British firm and their selection of DIB as the only company of any size capable of undertaking such a project. He nodded in agreement, turned around to my original contact and asked him whether two letters of agreement could be prepared within twenty-four hours. Prepared meant being cleared by the legal department which, as usual, represented the major time-consuming hurdle. The man said he would try and would telephone me later. We shook hands and parted.

The following morning two letters were delivered to my office. One covered the 4% required by my Iraqi associates and one covered the ½% required by us – we had beaten the deadline by a few hours. It was obvious that the letters were written by lawyers aware of the prohibitive laws of the Republic of Iraq, who had taken care to circumvent those laws.

I arranged an emergency meeting with my own lawyer and

showed him the two letters for his opinion. He confirmed that they were both valid and binding but expressed some unease regarding the term of the agreement, which stipulated one year renewable under certain circumstances. Also, he did not like the general nature of the letter to me and the gratuitous business of my being made responsible for arranging travel plans under the terms of the Hamdani agreement.

That notwithstanding, I coded a telex to Baghdad and told my people that the mission was accomplished and a telex should be sent to the DIB man immediately which, in its conclusion, should refer to past problems existing between DIB and Iraq being resolved amicably. I kept DIB informed and asked them to do the same for me.

The following morning I received a telex pre-dated by twenty-four hours, indicating that DIB was invited. I telephoned DIB immediately and asked for verification. My contact said he had not received the telex but asked me to stay on the telephone while he checked with the telex room. The message came back that a telex had just been received addressed to him and it included a friendly statement regarding previous problems between DIB and the Republic of Iraq. He was ecstatic. 'Sir, I will never forget this. We're in business – now our job is to get the sub-contractors and I am going to start work on it right away.'

With the telexed invitation in hand, a senior representative of DIB, whom we will call Richard Nye, went to the Iraqi Embassy in London to obtain a visa. Not surprisingly, instructions had been issued to the staff of the Embassy to facilitate the issuing of such a visa and it was granted within twenty-four hours. A message to DIB via us asked for their representative to be in Baghdad as soon as possible, and so he was – nine days from the day negotiations started with his company.

The situation in Baghdad was relatively easy. Our friends had identified Mr Nye to officials throughout the Ministries of Planning and Transport as a man who should be accommodated and helped. The various reports prepared by the consultants were given to him and clear instructions were issued to all concerned to pass on to him and his company all the information available. From day one it became apparent that the problem centred around one focal area: the size of the project and the marshalling of the staff by DIB and the various sub-contractors they selected to digest the masses of data available and come through with a proposal to the Iraqi Government as fast as possible.

Nye shuttled back and forth between London and Baghdad, contacting the various heads of committees, securing special permits to visit the sites and perusing tens of lengthy documents. DIB was proceeding to make a first-hand assessment of the project and competitors.

DIB's action in arranging the various sub-contractors was remarkable for its speed. In the building area they secured the co-operation of another major British construction company. In the areas pertaining to the procurement of steel and rail they reached a co-operation agreement with GKN. They even went beyond that to the more advanced elements – normally left until the last minute – such as the procurement of materials to go into the various small railway stops and stations and actually signed an agreement with a company making signalling equipment (so did we).

All of this they were doing on their own, while we were fulfilling our part of the bargain. This was to provide a secondary level of communications, acting parallel with the official one which fed them information daily. In other words, in addition to what they were being told officially, they were being given inside information by us which reflected the thinking of the higher levels of the Ministry of Planning and Ministry of Transport. Through the same sources, we received day-to-day bulletins on the competition which we daily passed on.

Three other countries (in projects of this size the company and country are one) were extremely interested in this project. India, already mentioned, had something to offer. The second was Yugoslavia which, though it had limited experience in that field, did have major construction companies and surplus labour. Besides, it was a fellow socialist country with ideological kinship to Iraq. Yugoslavia leaned on the goodwill of the Iraqi Government. The third candidate was Brazil, a surprise entry. The Brazilians, too, had a certain amount of expertise in the field, but, more intriguingly, their proposal suggested the possibility of barter. Brazil would build this project in return for Iraqi oil which they desperately needed.

None of these companies or countries had the support of anyone of the stature of Hamdani. None of the companies' 'Mr Big' or intermediary had the immunity to issue instructions to the various governmental departments equivalent to the one which helped DIB. None of the companies had DIB's reputation in the international construction field, nor did the companies proposed for sub-contracting have the reputation of the people selected by DIB.

Estimates of how long it would take to tender for this project varied from one to two years. The cost involved was very high and the figure most commonly quoted was £1,000,000 out of pocket, beside the time and effort of somewhere between thirty and fifty employees, most with senior staff classification.

DIB, as I have said, was desperate for the project. Staff were assigned to the job and found themselves surveying the western parts of Iraq, negotiating trails uninviting to even the most nomadic of Arabian peninsula tribes.

This project was going very well. In fact, everyone spoke of it as 'going through unless something disastrous takes place'. The something disastrous was to come out of the dark shadows of Baghdad soon enough and it assumed the personality of our roving skimmer. It was no other than our young Colonel Hamdar, the big project interceptor, the President's son-in-law. His addressing himself to the project was testimony to our prospects of success. It was as reassuring as the willingness of DIB and its various partners to invest the necessary money and time speculatively. This money was not refundable if they didn't win the contract. The competitors were less generous with both their time and their money.

The natural man for the skimmer to contact was the head of the DIB team in Baghdad, Nye himself. To contact him was easy because he and his team lived at the Baghdad Hotel. Soon enough, the initial meeting between Nye and the Colonel's representative took place. This was reported in full to DIB but was not reported to us at all. Characteristically, the demand was for 80% of all fees and commission earmarked for people who introduced the project to DIB. He did not ask nor did he care who they were. He did make it clear that denial of his request would harm DIB's chances of winning.

One should take into consideration that, of the four leading companies involved, DIB was an obvious favourite, though the

Yugoslavs and Brazilians were enthusiastic. The Colonel was chasing a winner.

The company's reaction to the initial request from the Colonel was to say no. This message was given to his people, again in dark corners of the Baghdad Hotel, with the necessary apologies. They had to refuse, they explained, because they were irrevocably committed to us. And, while they wished to accommodate the Colonel and were sure he was in a position to help them, the margin of profit was narrow and ruled out further payments on their part. Still, they offered to pay $5,000,000 instead of the eighty-odd he requested.

The dialogue between Nye and the Colonel's delegates continued. It climaxed in a meeting between Nye and the Colonel himself, where Nye explained in detail the company's point of view: extra commission to the level committed would make their offer totally uncompetitive and would most certainly lead to their elimination for being too expensive. The Colonel's retort was simple. He was aware of the details, he said, and was not asking for a new commission but was asking DIB to ask their present sponsors – us – to cede that part of the commission to him. He gave DIB two weeks in which to give him a final answer.

At this point DIB contacted me with the awesome details of the request. Staggered as I was by the development, I had no answer to offer except to contact my associates and promise to get back to DIB within forty-eight hours. I was spared the agony of transmitting this rather complicated request through coded telephone message to Baghdad because the people at the other end appeared to know all about it, and were ready with their answer. Their answer was a simple no, and it was not negotiable.

To avoid having to pass on this reply in all its baldness, I had a meeting with a member of the DIB board, gave him the message and solicited his advice as to what we should jointly do to diffuse the crisis. Our mutual concern was to arrive at a formula acceptable and beneficial to all. However, the DIB man, like his colleagues and myself, refused to consider adding another level of commission. To compound the problem, the Brazilian offer was beginning to appeal to a section of Iraqi officialdom.

DIB's hope rested on the fullness of detail of their plan and the implied quality of their work. However, none of this would be enough to offset a level of commission approaching $200,000,000. The DIB man appealed to me to petition my people to accept a fifty-fifty division of commission with the Colonel.

There were already signs that the Colonel was determined: numbers of the travelling survey team were delayed in Baghdad for five days while obtaining permits to visit the strategic area of Akashat. Others of them were being stopped in the streets and asked for their identity cards and were subjected to unreasonable quizzing as to their presence in Baghdad. Even the visas for those shuttling back and forth between Baghdad and London stopped being issued as easily as before.

The Hamdani people proved to be as stubborn as the Colonel. They had run into him before and had decided the time had come to draw the line. They believed that DIB would win the contract anyway. To them the Brazilians represented no threat because the people of the technical committee were on our side and judged the DIB offer to be infinitely superior. After all, Brazil's investment in preparing the offer was a small fraction of what DIB had already spent.

This final answer was relayed to DIB through channels in Baghdad and the issue was joined. There were those of us, myself included, who were convinced that the Colonel would do something drastic. Like all people in this business, he could not afford to lose face. His attack on this project had become well known to too many people. Giving in would mean his end as a roving skimmer.

Of all the people shuttling between London and Baghdad in connection with this project, the most peripheral was an Arab who represented the signalling company DIB had sub-contracted. This man and his company were introduced to DIB by us and accepted as part of the package.

This unfortunate man was selected by the Colonel and his dirty tricks team as the target to exemplify their determination to force DIB to co-operate with them. He was a small man in a small company; and because he was an Arab, harm done to him would not cause the same international stir as harm done to a European.

One day soon after our message of refusal reached the Colonel, this man was aboard a 'plane leaving Baghdad for London. The 'plane was full and the cabin staff were closing the doors of the aircraft to ready it for take-off when two civilian-dressed security men appeared and asked if a certain Mr Sami Abuljebin was aboard. He was paged on the public address system and the poor man meekly raised his hand and was asked to accompany the security men, who instructed the cabin staff to close the door and proceed with the flight.

Sami Abuljebin, forty-two, a small-time trader who had attended the High School of the American University of Beirut and depended on the favours of its more successful graduates to make a living, was escorted outside the terminal building of Baghdad Airport, put in a car and shot dead at point-blank range. The Colonel and his men murdered a totally innocent man to demonstrate that they meant business. For the sake of $80,000,000 they were willing to murder in broad daylight in the middle of the city of Baghdad.

Sami Abuljebin's death was not reported until two weeks after the event. The Director of National Security in Baghdad attributed death to a heart attack. An illiterate taxi driver was produced to tell how Mr Abuljebin died in his car. Why the news was kept for so long was not explained. Why involve the Chief of National Security and why not release the body to his mourning family?

Murder has a strange effect on people. Murder opens doors for more murder and it changes the rules of the game. The news of Sami's death sent shock waves through the DIB organisation and left me psychologically off-balance. I was ready to surrender rather than die.

DIB began to waver. They sent me a letter unilaterally cancelling our agreement. Our solicitors wrote back stating that unilateral action was not acceptable and we considered what the agreement actually meant.

Both agreements, the one for Hamdani and the one for my group, were still in my personal name. They had not been transferred out of my name as had been planned because of the confusion of the Colonel's request. I did not know whether the Colonel and his people knew this. However, it placed an additional burden on me and the fear that they would attempt to force me to sign the agreements over to them, or for that matter, make me cede the agreements and then kill me, was real. On the other hand, the only thing I was able to control was the ½% which belonged to me.

At that particular moment, I would very happily have signed my share away to the Colonel and his people but it was considerably short of what they wanted. Then it occurred to me to sign away 80% of the agreement without consulting anyone in Baghdad.

Doing this would not relieve me or absolve me of my responsibilities, it could only buy time to find a way out of the whole situation. There was also the hope that my associates would prove to be more reasonable than the Colonel's people – I knew them to be less violent.

My solicitors gave me no help. They did not consider the case a legal matter, were totally aghast at the tactics involved and made it plain they wanted out. My associates, while making all types of empty Arab promises about guaranteeing my protection in London, did nothing of the sort.

Fear produces its own phantoms. For a period of a month, while contemplating how best to cede the 80%, every driver, doorman, waiter – even people I had known for years – represented a would-be killer. I took to sleeping at friends' places, often inventing excuses for the purpose. The most common excuse was to drink too much and pretend I wasn't able to make it home.

Finally, I could take it no longer, so I decided to act. First I approached the Popular Front for the Liberation of Palestine and promised them the ½%, the part which belonged to my group, in full and total payment to them for protecting me – if the deal went through. My second course of action was to cede 80% of the 4% which belonged to my associates to the Colonel's people in full and final payment. This was to be done by message via DIB.

The PFLP people agreed to my proposal but this hardly made me a hero with their young ideologues. They wanted the money for the cause but it didn't alter their opinion of the corrupt would-be contributor. They agreed to do the job for the money, rather than for love of me. This agreement was reached with PFLP's Maisser Kubaa; whether George Habbash was aware of it I do not know to this day. The DIB people, in the person of Nye, were informed of my desire to cede US $80,000,000 to the Colonel and his people and the papers were sent to my lawyer to effect the legal transfer. DIB insisted there was no agreement to transfer. They had become convinced that the Colonel was above the law, even above Hamdani's law.

While all of this was going on the Colonel was progressing his own plans to eliminate DIB from the competition. This could not be done easily. DIB was well ahead. The Iraqi Government had made it discreetly known that they preferred a British company as a matter of policy. The plans and designs developed by DIB were totally acceptable to the technical committee and, since the Colonel has no official portfolio, he could hardly issue direct orders to the people in the Ministry of Planning and Transportation (the domain of his competition) asking them not to award the contract to the British company. Whatever had to be done to stop DIB getting the contract had to outweigh all these considerations. It had to be something that would justify awarding the prize contract of the railway building programme of the Republic of Iraq and the Middle East to an inferior company.

It is very hard for normal minds to dream up a disqualification powerful enough to overcome DIB's distinct lead. It is very hard for decent minds even to conceive of what happened. It is impossible for anything but an evil mind to want to be party to its invention. But then we are already acquainted with our Colonel's Mafia-style approach to murder in public places just to frighten people. So the Colonel's sordid imagination went to work and produced a plan sinister enough for the pages of a spy thriller.

The Colonel contacted the Brazilians and struck a deal with them. This was easy because the Brazilians had all but given up on their chances, knowing how elaborately prepared the DIB offer was. Any promise to help them produced written promises of reward. No one else had asked to represent them. Having secured the co-operation of the Brazilians, the Colonel turned his attention to DIB.

Surely something could be done to eliminate them from competition. Obviously they were true Brits and the killing of someone 'connected' to them did not frighten them. Whatever was done had to be done to DIB, and it had to be aimed directly at discrediting and eliminating the company.

Dick Nye, the innocent down-to-earth engineer, a decent, direct, middle-aged man from the Midlands, had good reason to think that he was approaching the height of his career. He firmly believed that he would be the project manager on this major job, and that it would catapult him into a position on the DIB board.

He worked a sixteen-hour day, with unfailing dedication, shuttling his people from one corner of that ghastly blank that is Western Iraq to another, surveying the unsurveyable and microscopically examining every detail of the proposal that was being handed to the Iraqis. He returned to Iraq four days before the finished offer was to be given to the Ministry of Planning. It was to be carried in a car guarded by two others for reasons of security. It comprised thousands upon thousands of pages of maps and text.

Dick Nye arrived at the Baghdad Hotel with every expectation of capturing a prize construction project. It had taken ten months to put the offer together. Though, for reasons difficult to understand, he failed to advise the Colonel of my offer to cede him 4%, he had no idea of my connection with the Liberation Front, nor of the steps I had taken in that direction. He still thought he had a winner and counted on settling the commission problem later.

At 11.00 the following morning four security men in civilian clothes broke into the Baghdad Hotel and asked for Mr Richard Nye. Dick Nye was having a cup of coffee in the lobby and he was called over by a porter. When he approached the security men, one of them pulled an identity badge from his pocket and said, 'Mr Nye?' 'Yes.' 'Sir, you are under arrest for espionage activities against the interests of the Republic of Iraq.' He was taken from the hotel directly to the maximum security prison in Baghdad.

No committee, no ministry, no collection of people, however brave, committed or convinced, no amount of inherent goodwill could possibly overcome the stigma of an espionage charge. Hamdani vanished in thin air. He ran away.

The moment Dick Nye was charged with spying was the moment DIB lost the contract. Of course, his assistant delivered the tender documents but the committee never reviewed them and the contract was destined for the Brazilians and our roving skimmer.

Dick Nye spent four years in an Iraqi prison. He was released by the intercession of King Hussein of Jordan. My Liberation Front protectors left me as soon as the news came out that the contract was to go to the Brazilians (and, surprisingly, Indians). My Iraqi associates, having discovered that I was in the process of ceding the agreement to the Colonel, severed their business connections with me. What's more, they still owe me $480,000. Hamdani was executed two years later for reasons totally unconnected with this.

The roving skimmer won. Sami Abuljebin is dead. Dick Nye will never be the same again. I am poorer, wiser and perhaps a little more careful. The Liberation Front proved that it can be bought for the right price. Almost every imaginable element of intrigue seemed to surface in this deal. Perhaps it goes to prove the old adage that 'the bigger it is the more dangerous it is'. The size of this deal made murder possible.

Had the Colonel waited a while, he would have had DIB. Our agreements with them were scheduled to expire in two months.

11

••

'Either You Endeavour or
You Guarantee'

All too many people, with little knowledge and strong opinions, have prophesied a Communist Middle East since the Suez Crisis in 1956. Those who know the Arab Middle East well, who understand the independence of the Arab mind and its inability to develop serious attachments to alien ideologies, find these prophets of gloom and doom ignorant and annoying.

Some Westerners with right-wing leanings use their pessimism as an excuse to urge military occupation of the region, to guarantee its continuation as a Western preserve. Others genuinely believe that the Arabs are incapable of managing their own affairs, and that outsiders should do it for them.

In reality, Communism is not only unable to capture the imagination of the Arabs in general, its Russian exporters have consistently offended the sensibilities of an all-important section of Arab decision makers: army officers. The Russians have suffered serious reverses in Egypt, the Sudan, Syria and Iraq. These failures have never received the attention they deserve – certainly not from the right-wing press and its gurus, charter members of the 'there goes the Middle East' club. Had they received the proper exposure, we would know that army officers were behind most of them.

This is the story of Iraq's first major arms deal with the West. One which broke Russia's monopoly as the country's sole supplier of military hardware – a position which granted the Russians political influence. It demonstrates the fragility of Russian/Arab

120

relations and the disaffection of the officer corps with everything Russian.

The Iraqis are viewed by many, including Western intelligence sources, as the Prussians of the Middle East. They have a military tradition which is longer than most and, excepting the Israelis, their generalship and training appear superior to others. The Iraqi foot soldier is less fun-loving, more serious and educated than his Egyptian and Syrian counterparts. Their air force has been in existence for fifty years, and was the only one successfully to penetrate the Israeli defence net. A little-known but important reason for the envied Iraqi Air Force expertise is their training which was, and continues to be, British. Even the most troubled times didn't interfere with this aspect of Anglo-Iraqi relations and, as I am writing, over one hundred and fifty Iraqi Air Force pilots are receiving training at the facilities of ABMTM Ltd (Association of British Machine Tool Manufacturers) in Cambridge. There is good reason for this to continue. The Iraqis have acquitted themselves well against the US-trained Iranians and would have done better if President Saddam Hussein, like many heads of state, didn't have the weakness of playing general.

The Iraqi officer's personal empathy has always been with the Western democracies. His Moslem background and British training both contribute to this, and it is reinforced by the austere remoteness of the Russian officers sent to Iraq to educate him in the use of their equipment. During 1975 it became apparent to the rulers of Iraq that Russia was holding back on supplying them with its most sophisticated military equipment, particularly advanced fighter and bomber aircraft. Until then, they naively believed in Russian friendship. This Russian betrayal soon became the worst-kept secret in Baghdad. The Iraqis complained, without success.

To Iraq's generals, the quarrel between their government and Russia represented an opportunity to pay back the humourless Russians for their patronising attitudes, and they hit back with lethal deliberateness. Capitalising on their leaders' disaffection, they recommended the purchase of an Anglo-French fighter-bomber, then one of the most advanced aircraft in the world and one which met Iraq's need to protect itself against both Iran and Israel.

This was a move which went beyond arms sales to a reorientation in the political direction of the country. This suggestion was approved with amazing alacrity by an Iraqi leadership whose frustration and anger with Russia had been on the rise. They wanted an alternate source of military hardware which would lessen their dependence on Russia and give them political room for manoeuvre.

The Iraqi-Russian dispute and subsequent decision were translated into a request (from Hamdani's office) for me to begin unofficial negotiations with a British aircraft manufacturer to buy the fighter-bomber. It reached me two days after the Iraqi leadership's milestone decision. My exact mission was to determine this company's possible interest in fulfilling Iraqi requirements for a fighter-bomber and to secure a 6% commission agreement for my Iraqi associates.

A London friend of mine gave me the name of the company's director of the military aircraft division, John Hannay, whom I telephoned, telling him my version of the Baghdad story: not that the decision was already made, but that 'our people' could help make it. His answers were polite but non-committal until I mentioned the number of aircraft needed; sixty (£200,000,000 worth). All pretences of disinterest vanished and the man's personal enthusiasm surfaced. He promised an answer after consulting his colleagues on the board.

Two days later the company confirmed its interest in working with us, but cautioned against too much optimism because of the unlikelihood of the British Government, then led by Harold Wilson, approving a sale to Iraq. At this point, I mentioned the 6% commission and the need for an agreement. He thought 6% too high but once again promised a quick answer. Again the reply was positive and there was a promise that a written confirmation would follow a meeting at the company's London office.

John Hannay is a model RAF officer and one of the finest gentlemen I have ever met. When I met him I gave him a full briefing on all I knew and undertook to arrange a meeting for him with my contact in Baghdad as soon as I had received a written agreement. I gave him the name of the company to which the agreement should be assigned, Arab Resources Management (ARM) of Beirut, Lebanon. I declined to explain who and what Arab Resources Management were, and Hannay assured me that the agreement was being prepared by lawyers and promised to query the Foreign Office on their attitude towards Iraq.

My contact in Baghdad was delighted with the progress I had made but annoyed at the delay in processing the agreement. He was doing his best to delay the arrival in London of an Iraqi Air Force delegation whose job was to make the 'official' enquiry to the company. Danger loomed. If the delegation arrived and made direct contact before a signed agreement was in our hands, then the company could do without us.

In a few days, a proposed agreement was received from the company. However, another hitch in the way of finalising it developed because I couldn't sign on behalf of Arab Resources Management. The time for Hannay to meet Dr Ramzi A. Dalloul had come. The latter, a confidant and advisor to Iraqi Minister of Planning, Adman Hamdani, was the Chairman of ARM. He acted on behalf of Hamdani and others and the 6% commission covered all people involved, myself included.

As stipulated, the agreement was deposited in a Swiss bank for safe keeping. The company was haunted by the spectre of a Lockheed-type scandal, which they attributed to the naiveté of the Americans. To them, selling military aircraft was the same as selling cars but they still craved secrecy, insisting on calling the agreement 'a consultancy'. The agreement could be examined by either party any time but it took both sides to withdraw it from the bank's safe deposit.

Much to my surprise, the initial response from the Foreign Office arrived before the Iraqi Air Force delegation did. Her Majesty's Government, according to the company, 'would view with favour' such a request by the Iraqi Government. This was too good to be true and an important step towards encouraging the Iraqi Government and officers to maintain their anti-Russian decision.

The euphoria enveloping the intermediary group all the way to Baghdad (£12,000,000 worth of it) vanished into thin air when the Iraqi delegation made known the type of agreement they would require. Purchasing the 'planes and training the pilots was only a first step. They wanted a British Government 'guarantee of uninterrupted flow of spare parts under all conditions'. Anxious to win the £200,000,000 contract, Her Majesty's Government wrote via the aircraft manufacturers stating that they would 'endeavour to guarantee' because they were not a company but a government. In reply, the head of the Iraqi delegation snapped at Hannay, 'My English is not good, but either you endeavour or you guarantee,' and with that he packed his bags and announced his departure for sunny Baghdad. For someone who had until then used a translator, his English was excellent.

The atmosphere of crisis was suffocating. I was seeing £12,000,000 slip through our fingers and was in constant touch with the company and Baghdad, trying to reconcile the two governments' points of view. The company was with us all the way, but there was not a great deal they could do.

One way of circumventing British Government stubbornness was to have the French co-manufacturers do the sale. But the Iraqi reply was full of derision. It referred to spare parts made for 'plane sections and engine, both obtainable in Britain only. Besides, they wanted the British-made navigation system. Compared to the company I was behaving rationally, for their second suggestion reeked of desperation. Why not leak the story to labour unions who needed jobs in the aircraft industry?

This would put pressure on Prime Minister Wilson – the union might even call a strike. Baghdad's response to this suggestion was a model of third-world smugness. It said, 'Iraq, which resents interference in its internal affairs, would never knowingly interfere in the internal affairs of another country.'

I kept pleading with the company to think of a way out of the impasse. They kept pressurising the Foreign Office, who wouldn't move. The overriding question was whether this would so discourage the Iraqis as to throw them back into the arms of Russia. One excitement with the arms deal transcended the £12,000,000; we were party to an historical occasion.

Iraq did not go back to the Russians. Dalloul, whom I always suspected of having motives beyond money, helped push the Iraqis towards the French in the form of Dassault's Mirage F1 'plane. They didn't need much pushing. Instead of returning to Baghdad, the Iraqi delegates had gone to Paris and M. Dassault. When the guarantee question was presented to Dassault he had the French Government sign a document in twenty-four hours.

Difficulties with the Mirage F1 purchase appeared later on. The

Iraqis, for reasons still unknown to me, suspected the French of overcharging them by £2,000,000 an aircraft. This time Dalloul's message to me bridged the distance between intermediary and espionage work. 'Drop whatever you are doing,' he screamed, 'and find out what the bastards charged other countries. You have unlimited expenses, use them to bribe, buy or bully anyone but get me the prices at which the French sold the F1 to others. Remember, I need it broken down because the extras, particularly the electronic gear, make a lot of difference.'

It was like going from the fryingpan of a rigid, unimaginative British Foreign Office to the fire of the slippery French. The Institute of Strategic Studies, an obvious source for this type of information, wouldn't help. Whatever contacts I had with intelligence establishments wanted more in return for their help than I was willing to offer.

I remember making an agreement to see a CIA type in a small Knightsbridge pub. Unhappily I ran into a boring American investment banker who kept talking to me about his bonus. Little did he know I was there to rescue a commission of £12,000,000 and perhaps the balance of power in the Middle East.

My CIA chum recommended I tap the Peace Institute in Stockholm. They kept thorough files, he advised. In return for that I gave him the background on the deal. I hoped Washington would lean on Paris to stop its silly money tricks. What was at stake was bigger than money, we agreed.

My problem was how to get the Peace Institute files. For that I bribed the correspondent of an American weekly. The money was good. This young man went to Stockholm and came back with the prize; he had copied all the price data they had on Mirage F1 sales. The Institute files were complete.

Dalloul, who by then had been elevated to the post of advisor to the Iraqi Government and was acting in this official capacity, met me in Paris. He was astounded. The Iraqis were right. The French had overpriced the 'plane.

The Iraqis got Dalloul's report and began to stall. Chirac, the then French Prime Minister, was to visit them in a short while. This was part of the new opening to the West. It was an opportunity to pressure him while he was on their turf. Chirac was well received in Baghdad. He dealt with Saddam Hussein, then

Vice-President, but the obvious power behind the throne. When the time came to discuss business Chirac asked about the Mirage F1 deal. Saddam Hussein pushed a large sheet of paper in front of him analysing the sale of the F1 to various countries. It showed an obvious attempt by the French to overcharge the Iraqis.

The document was examined by the imperturbable Chirac with the help of an aide. He didn't question the figures but volunteered – on the spot – a reduction of $1,750,000 in the price of each 'plane. Saddam Hussein accepted, and the gentlemen shook hands. The deal was happily concluded by the same Iraqi delegation which had visited London and Paris a month earlier. Unlike other Arabs the Iraqis don't like to squander their money.

Later Saddam Hussein was to learn about Dalloul's commission agreement. To him this was betrayal because he considered Dalloul a trusted advisor who received a healthy retainer. He expelled Dalloul from Iraq, claimed and got the commission from the French.

As I write, there is news of the use of the F1s against Iran. For a change, the French kept their word and they continue to send spare parts to Iraq. How much my efforts helped and whether Washington ever put pressure on them or not is something I will never know.

Dalloul now lives in London, surrounding himself with secrecy and bodyguards. Hannay runs his own consulting services, my American journalist friend is in New York and I am writing this book. The winner is Saddam Hussein. He got his 'planes at the lowest price possible without paying commission and broke Russia's hold on his army and country. It is not difficult to identify the losers.

12

* * *

'Stealing the Moon'

'It's like walking through a minefield – and if you make it safely to the other side then the rewards are staggering.' Thus did one leading Saudi intermediary sum up the nature of his business.

Of course, life is made easier, and richer, if you have a mine detector, and know the lay of the land and the clear passages – i.e. if you have inside information on the decision makers in a deal. Occasionally an intermediary is in the ideal position of being one of the decision makers himself.

If an intermediary can corner the whole market, or a specialised segment of it, in one product, he can grow ever richer as follow-up orders come through. Here are two unusual success stories of men who had special help and set up quasi monopolies.

Rami Abu Karim is a senior intelligence officer in the Iraqi Secret Service. Like many such officers, he is a former journalist, having worked as a reporter on *Al Distour* news magazine. He was originally recruited by the Ministry of Information for his supposed knoweldge of domestic and international affairs. After years of service, Abu Karim was promoted to a senior untitled position where he is in charge of liaison with Iraqi intelligence officers attached to diplomatic missions in Europe. To my knowledge these are highly professional, dedicated young ideologues who are above reproach.

His appointment was an odd one. Darker than most Iraqis, his command of English amusingly poor, Abu Karim is 5 feet 6 inches tall, shaves his head Yul Brynner style, sports a large snout and gigglingly calls himself Kojak. He does look a bit like Telly Savalas, but much more resembles a Red Indian chief in an old-fashioned western. At any rate, he is easily identifiable.

Abu Karim needed a cover for his constant travelling in Europe to stay in touch with Iraqi operatives, and the Iraqis created a film importing company as a front for him. He imports film for use in Iraqi cinemas and on TV. The Cinema and Television Establishment is part of the Ministry of Information, Abu Karim's employer. It's a good cover, for it allows him to roam around the countries from which Iraq imports film: the UK, Germany, France, etc. Equipped with import licences and ready cash (both usually difficult to obtain), Abu Karim was well received by international film makers wishing to enter a hitherto unknown territory.

What Abu Karim does is simple enough. He buys rubbishy old films at very low prices and sells them to the Cinema and TV establishment at a profit of 150%–500%. He uses the facilities of the establishment (telex, etc.) for communications, has film shipped collect on Iraqi Airways (a privilege originally granted for the transmission of information gathered) and has adopted the role of protecting Iraq from Zionist film makers (anyone who refuses to co-operate with him is a Zionist). With these facilities, and his freedom to travel in Europe, he is beyond competition. What competitors there were got an inkling of what Abu Karim was all about and disappeared into thin air.

Iraq has three television stations including an educational one. It has hundreds of cinemas. Abu Karim shamelessly accounts for 90% of film imports (rentals). This means about $6,000,000–$10,000,000 worth of film imports a year – close to treble that in profits. This kind of regular income makes Abu Karim Film Distribution one of the most profitable companies in Iraq, and Abu Karim (its sole employee) one of the most successful intermediaries in the Middle East.

Unhappily for him, the old maxim of money corrupting has proved true. Because of his 'immunity' he has taken to deferring payment on his imports, then not paying. He doesn't return film rented for one- or two-time use and his Zionist blackmail has become too widespread to be effective. He is not satisfied with his millions a year.

As a result of his greed, and his attempts to cheat not only Iraq but film companies as well, he is now hounded by several law suits and his mobility around Europe is limited, which damages his usefulness as an intelligence gatherer. Yet his superiors seem to have accepted whatever explanations he has given them for the curtailment of his movements. And as far as the film business is concerned the lack of mobility doesn't matter; he represents the world's leading film studios and the money keeps rolling in.

Film and television is an unusual line of business for an intermediary. My second success story concerns an operator in a much more likely area – armament. TS is a Palestinian living in Dubai. He comes from a small village outside Jerusalem and was a minor member of the Jordanian Foreign Service. In that post he befriended a number of army officers, including the Director of Procurement and Purchasing for Dubai, one of the Emirates. Wishing to exploit his connections, TS set up a small company to sell soft military wares; tents, boots, uniforms, etc.

At first TS had no pretensions. A good-looking man of about forty, he suffered from a stutter and a fondness for eye-troubling colour combinations – yellow shirts and black jackets, brown alligator shoes with pale blue trousers, etc. His lack of style made him visible a mile away.

To start with he had little or no money to bribe anyone with. But he turned his little Dubai apartment into a sort of small night club where army officers stayed until the early hours, listening to music and drinking Black Label whisky. He also established connections with a few Far Eastern suppliers of soft military goods. His friends helped him and he did the odd deal or two a year which earned him a good living.

During one of TS's visits to London, fortune appeared in the person of MF, a retired RAF wing-commander and a hero of the Battle of Britain. A gentleman of the old school with impeccable credentials and manners, MF had little in common with TS. But TS is a good talker, and seemed to know the right people. The wing-commander was seduced.

MF had close connections with a German arms maker, one of the leading international makers of 20mm ammunition for anti-aircraft guns. This company had heard that Dubai wanted their product, and needed an intermediary to promote their position.

TS and MF met their representative at the London Hilton and signed an agreement whereby the company would pay them 14% commission on all business done with Dubai. With this secured, TS hurried back to Dubai to lobby on their behalf.

His small, after-hours group were an indiscreet lot, and Black Label tended to loosen their tongues further. Yes, Dubai was indeed in need of some 20mm annunition. And since samples would be tested before such materials were bought, the cheap Far Eastern suppliers would be swiftly disqualified for poor quality goods. Yes, this little group of influential officers would advocate going with the Germans; it was a good company.

TS was back in London like a shot. He provided all the inside information necessary to go after the job. And TS had been promised up-to-date information if and when the situation changed.

An authorised company representative flew to Dubai with company stationery and settled in at the local Sheraton Hotel. He kept in constant touch with TS who waited until the last minute, when all other offers were in, before advising on how to organise the winning offer.

The Germans got the contract and it was the first of many. TS used the same successful approach. The average commission was about £800,000 for each order and there were no less than six.

TS's helpers didn't do what they did for money. They helped him because they enjoyed his late-hours bar which soon enough acquired 'barmaids' specifically flown from London. They led him through the minefield, showed him the lay of the land and cleared his path. The whole operation cost him about £10,000 and a week's work.

It didn't stop there. TS's late-night spot became one of the most famous clearing-houses in Dubai. He made tens of millions of pounds for himself and more for a number of major international companies.

TS comes from the biblical village of Bethany where I was born. The last time I saw him he was trying to sell a sophisticated radar system which identified friendly 'planes from hostiles ones. A far

130

cry from the Bethany of our boyhood. I never think of him without smiling, for he reminds me of a story about our not-very-distant forebears.

In 1932, my grandfather, a judge of the High Islamic Court and a lecturer in Arabic literature at the Arab College, was resident chief of Bethany. One night in May some of the villagers, led by the Sadawi brothers – TS's father and three uncles – attacked the village of Abu Dis, across the valley. Hearing the shooting, Grandfather despatched one of my uncles to find out what was going on.

My uncle returned helpless with laughter, and explained that the Sadawis were furious with the people of Abu Dis because they had 'stolen the moon'. The moon, which usually rose over Bethany, had risen that evening over Abu Dis, and the Sadawis were determined to recover her.

Grandfather sent a messenger (there were no telephones) to the chief of Abu Dis saying that the Sadawis were nuts, and pleading that the matter be contained. He sent another to the Sadawis ordering their retreat.

The Sadawis were summoned to explain their precipitous action. There they all were, including my friend's father, complaining about the underhandedness of Abu Dis. My grandfather listened to their ignorant pleas without a smirk. He extracted a pledge of good behaviour and asked them to return in two days.

He consulted the astronomy books in the Arab College, and learned the pattern of the moon's orbit. When the Sadawis came back to see him he was all ready. The moon belonged to them at certain times of the year and to Abu Dis the rest of the time. This, my grandfather insisted, was his final judgement and was not subject to appeal.

TS has come a long, unhappy way since the stealing of the moon. I estimate that he made $40,000,000 in 1981 and 1982. But he couldn't cope with the changes such wealth made in his life. He took to having his nails manicured twice a week and his hair fluffed daily. He spent more and more time in London and complained about how drab Dubai was. Eventually he gave up Dubai and the things which had made him successful.

13

How to Lose a Deal

Any business deal anywhere in the world can be lost for straight-forward business reasons – prices are too high, a company is inadequately qualified, an offer does not match the specifications required. But in the Middle East deals are also lost for reasons often unrelated to business. Intermediaries see huge deals, and large commissions, slip away from them all too often.

One painful way for an intermediary to lose a contract is when a Middle Eastern government subordinates business to politics. A government will occasionally give a contract to a French company because they are French, and not becuase they made the cheapest or best offer. This happens because the French government voted 'the right way' at the United Nations or, as in the case with Iraq now, the French supplied the government in power with arms when the British, Americans, Germans and others would not. Alternatively, the government could be paving the way for a special relationship, making a gesture of goodwill in anticipation of reciprocal action.

An able intermediary and/or his boss should be able to predict such tilts and prejudices and use them to advantage by getting a French company to work with them. Certainly he should be able to avoid wasting time and effort by promoting the 'wrong' national-ity. He must have a nose for which countries are in fashion at any point, and a talent for predicting changes. Fashions are different in each country. The US has always been fashionable in Saudi Arabia but its position changes constantly in other countries.

You can also lose deals by being inflexible with skimmers; and

132

you must be in a position to judge whether a skimmer can stop or damage a deal. If the skimmer's ability to influence a deal is beyond the intermediary's control then he should, within reason, be accommodated. And as fast as possible, because once a skimmer begins to undo a deal it's very hard for him to stop. The case of the young Colonel's meddling in the Iraqi railway construction contract has demonstrated this.

Vicious, cut-throat methods are required to stop an otherwise successful offer. Perhaps a whisper in the right ears that a certain company is 'suspected of having Israeli ties'. This happened with the US electronic giant Honeywell, which was blacklisted on a false charge, then reinstated. Perhaps a company will be disqualified on a minor technicality which would normally have made little difference. Or a skimmer may pressurise a bank into delaying a company's letter of guarantee, or pretending that the company's documents, or some of them, had been lost. And of course the obvious way, if the skimmer has sufficient clout, is simply to order officials, without giving any reason or needing to, not to award the contract to the unco-operative company.

All other non-business ways of losing a contract fall into two general categories: either too much commission is built in to the offer, or legal problems arise after one side tries to cheat the other.

High commissions increase prices. If a country wants to build a bridge and all five companies competing can build it equally efficiently, clearly the price is the determining factor. The commission must therefore remain low to keep the price low. If it is high the deal will be lost.

On the other hand, specialised situations where a unique product or service is required and can only be supplied by one company, can bear high commissions because there are no competitors. President Saddam Hussein bought US-made M16 rifles for his personal guards on the open market. They could not buy them from the manufacturer. The commission was a hefty 25% of value because there was only one make. This usually obtains with high technology, electronic and armament companies.

Demands for unreasonably high commissions are sometimes made from pure greed. Even people who should know better often ask for a commission 'higher than the traffic can bear' hoping to get away with it.

Commissions also soar unacceptably high when too many people are involved in a deal. If one intermediary uses another to secure the co-operation of a particular company, then the second intermediary has to be satisfied too. From the other side, we act on behalf of many companies who once signed agreements with ineffectual agents, and found they had to co-operate with an intermediary and the official agent, again creating another layer of commission. Sometimes a company employee will intrude, wishing to be part of the intermediary team under the umbrella of Mr Big. Thus the man recommending that the company use a particular intermediary is doing so because the latter has become his partner. This situation, too, pushes up the level of commission. And there are situations where Mr Big isn't as influential as he pretended, and has to take care of too many officials to buy the deal, inflating the size of the commission.

The legal complications which scotch deals usually result either from one side reneging on an agrement, or from a company using all available weasels to avoid paying commissions. This is considerably more complex than the too-much-commission syndrome.

One bald and incontrovertible fact: if a company wishes to avoid paying commission, it can. It doesn't matter how elaborate, watertight and legally binding an agreement they sign with an intermediary. Going to court, supposedly the last resort, is no help, because legal suits mean publicity, which means the whole deal collapses, which nobody wants. And it reflects more on the intermediary than the company. While some governments' attitudes betray a *de facto* acceptance of the commission system, no government can appear to condone it to the world community in the form of intermediary (as distinct from agent) activity.

Companies, some of which are particularly adept at trickery, will try to cancel an agreement or reduce commission after they are well into a deal, usually after they have exhausted Mr Big's ability to help them. A company will sign or agree to anything to obtain inside information from the intermediary and his Mr Big which will put them in a favourable position to win their contract. They become less eager after things start to go their way.

The first thing many companies do when they want to get out of the intermediary agreement is to petition Mr Big's team to reduce their commission. The company always claims that such a reduction is necessary because of the competition. Periodically, this is accepted by both sides, the commission is reduced accordingly and difficulties are avoided. Most often the company's pleas are turned down, which is when the legal fun and games begin.

In trying to cancel an agreement, companies behave according to their nationality. Koreans and Japanese write informing their sponsor of their decision. They give no explanation. Germans, Swiss and Swedes support the decision with a detailed analysis of the situation. Letters to the same effect from French companies are confusing and unclear. The British are normally very apologetic but their move is necessitated by 'broad consideration', and the American decision is always the result of 'reconsideration'. To cancel an agreement altogether, companies, whatever their nationality, exploit every imaginable loophole in the document though, in truth, no loophole is needed.

Usually they find one in the duration of the agreement. Very few agreements are open-ended; most stipulate a term of effectiveness, supposedly renewable if certain conditions are met. When a company is disinclined to renew an agreement, they will always find a way of claiming that those conditions were not met. After all, the 'conditions' are vague and subject to varied interpretation. For example, a company may claim that a contract stipulating 'facilitation of travel' has been broken because their representative wasn't met at the airport.

Not renewing an agreement, whether for a just or unjust cause, can do considerable harm to everyone involved. If an agreement is for a year, and the contract is not awarded within that time, failure to renew means that Mr Big and the intermediary will get nothing for their pains. Though it is not productive, Mr Big and his team will more often than not try to torpedo the deal, rather than simply accept non-renewal. Again, because of the noise level, everybody loses.

Other excuses used by companies to cancel an agreement include the 'sudden' awareness of the laws of the country where the contract is to take place. Our old friends laws 8 and 52 in Iraq not only prohibit the use of intermediaries, they make it an offence punishable by death. Companies know this very well before signing an agreement; but prior knowledge doesn't stop them from quoting such laws to cancel the agreement unilaterally. They always claim that they have 'belatedly become aware that the Laws of the Republic of Iraq prohibit such an activity'.

The antidote is the same. Their ex-sponsors will do their best to punish them by losing them the contract. After all, Mr Big must always demonstrate that companies cannot undermine him. Otherwise he becomes fair game and other companies working with him will try the same ploy.

I have said before that intermediaries draft agreements carefully to circumvent the law. Sometimes these dodges can be used against them. A US construction company signed an agreement to pay an intermediary and his master 4½% of the value of a contract to build a ring road around northern Iraq. The total value was estimated at $2,000,000,000. Because of laws 8 and 52, the agreement expressed 'willingness to pay $90,000,000 in return for logistical services including the making of hotel and travel reservations'. When the company decided to cancel the agreement the intermediary was helpess; he had never made travel or hotel reservations. In this case the sponsors failed to stop the company, which won the project without paying the commission.

An agreement can be effectively reneged on by bringing it under US law, which prohibits agreements that include 'questionable payments that may reach government officialdom'. The only difference between US and Iraqi law is that the US Government is likely to applaud the reneging company and support it in squeezing the intermediary team out of the picture. The Iraqis punish both.

If a company manages to reach higher than its sponsor, this undermines their agreement and very often leads to its cancellation. The French are best at this because their government often acts as their promoter. A few years ago Airbus Industries appointed a sales agent in Iraq, the agreement between them stipulating a hefty 5% commission on all sales to that country. When Premier Chirac of France visited Iraq, the Iraqi Prime Minister told him that Iraq would buy eight aircraft from Airbus. Chirac reported this to the company, who in turn wrote to the agent saying that the deal had been done prime minister to prime minister; no sales effort had been expended by him, and they saw no need to pay commission. They didn't and he had to accept.

Any row over an agreement causes bad publicity. The deal in question is lost, but so is the intermediary's reputation with other companies, other intermediaries, and the establishment in his country of influence. Besides, companies can rest assured that the spirit if not the letter of the law will always support them.

Most of the pay-outs under discussion involve hundreds of thousands, if not millions, of pounds or dollars. Any company can safely assume that no British judge making about £50,000 a year would ever award millions to an intermediary as due recompense for his work, or, for that matter, for what he considers a highly questionable if not altogether illegal activity. This regardless of the written content of an agreement. As one British company man told me when I threatened legal action, 'Go ahead, the little old judge is on our side.' I had to settle for what the company offered.

Some companies' legal problems are of their own making and do not result from their desire to terminate or amend a contract with a promoter. They can originate in the company's own deviousness. Companies will use two intermediaries operating at different levels without telling either. They do this to guarantee all-round support (e.g. on both the technical and political sides). When this is discovered, the company alienates one party or the other, if not both. In such cases, the law must sometimes be brought in to determine who is truly the company's representative, with all the attendant bad publicity and damage.

Yet for every two – or six – deals lost, there will be one that comes off with spectacular success. Despite the fact that his alliance with any company is likely to be an unholy one, and despite his uneasy standing vis-à-vis the law, the intermediary is alive and well in the Middle East.

14

In Praise of Equality

I would like to expand on one not-so-obvious aspect of the intermediary's role – the nature of his relationship with his master. I said in Chapter One that this is primarily a business relationship, which has its more personal side. This is certainly the case; but what brings the partnership into being in the first place?

Born and bred an Arab, but having lived away from the Middle East for most of my life, I am in a good position to observe the patterns of behaviour on the intermediary scene. There is no social mobility in the Middle East; a businessman can never aspire to be in the same class as a prince. But within these strict limitations partnerships are formed by equals; people with the same preferences, the same sense of humour, etc. And there is no doubt that there is a special sense of camaraderie, a hidden understanding between an intermediary and his master. There may be little or no love or respect there, but their intercommunication is on a special level.

In a group of ten or so people surrounding an Arab decision maker at any time, one can always tell which is his intermediary. There is something between the two which is completely theirs. Not that Mr Big cannot recognise that others may be cleverer and more able than his chosen henchman. It simply doesn't matter. Their relationship is more than personal servitude, greater than the intermediary's ability to negotiate with companies and translate the outside world to his boss. It is higher than discretion and personal attention. It is anchored in basic chemistry which makes one man willing to be led, used and very often abused by another, yet the partnership survives to the benefit of both. The name-calling and resentments may be there but they are subordinated to a mutual need, which is supported by their special ability to communicate.

This is a long way of saying that intermediates are not necessarily the most able and intelligent people in the world. They are, however, fortunate enough – and instinct has something to do with it – to have found mental and spirituals equals in high places.

We have already heard about TS in Dubai (see Chapter 12). This man set up different partnerships with six directors of the various departments of the armed forces (Procurement, Training, Organisation and Armament, Naval Force, Air Defences and Coastal Defences). In time, he added the Chief of Staff and his deputy and his monopoly of influence could only be broken when deals were done state to state, for example when French President Giscard D'Estaing sold F1 Mirage 'planes.

Our friend's basic qualification, the one which allowed him to create this elaborate set-up, was his similarity to the people in power. He was and is their equal. Though he comes from a different country, their taste in clothes (bright and showy), movies (sob stories), drinking (Black Label whisky), women (dizzy blondes), food (rice in tomato paste) and cars (huge, ornate American ones) is the same. Even what they read – when they do – is the same (French romantic novels). These common grounds are seldom mentioned directly, yet they constitute an unbreakable bond between them.

Apart from these preferences, they share a vast appetite for money. When people have so much in common, when there is so much agreement, communication is easy, even about the illegal and forbidden.

Prince Mohamad bin Abdel Aziz, King Fahd's elder brother, and the man who should be king if he didn't drink so heavily, is the largest seller of Saudi Arab oil on the international spot market. His intermediaries are his equals: crude, basic people with little to prepare them for their role as international traders in the world's most important commodity.

Some of them travel with crumpled pieces of paper with Mohamad's personal stamp on it offering hundreds of thousands, if not millions, of barrels of oil to would-be buyers. Dismissing them as 'too primitive to be true', some oil men missed their big chances while others, more current with what makes an intermediary, dealt with them and made fortunes.

The men around King Hussein of Jordan are his type, sophisticated and worldly. Their suits are made in London's fabled Savile Row, they frequent social clubs and posh restaurants, avoid ordinary night clubs and rice and tomato paste, speak impeccable English and don't go very far without consulting an international law firm like Coudert Frères or Clifford-Turner.

A former Chief of Staff of the Jordanian Army retired and decided to become an arms dealer. The man's position as Chief of Staff owed as much to his tribal background as his talents. His tribe supported Hussein and its support was important.

The man's first act as an arms dealer was to call on King Hussein to solicit help. After all, who knew better the needs of the Jordanian Army. Yet Hussein turned his back without hesitation. King Hussein rightly didn't wish the man to represent him in the international arms market. The man was backward, indiscreet, lacking in linguistic capability and mastery of English. He had been Chief of Staff for a good reason: he could not represent Hussein as an arms dealer.

One of my cousins does considerable business in Qatar. His bosses are a collection of polite, decent folks who swear by him. They telephone him almost daily, though he lives in Washington DC and they in Qatar. They travel, holiday and do business together though I don't believe there is a single legal document binding them.

My cousin and his chief benefactor were in London and invited me to dinner. I had forgotten how giggly my cousin is. His constant ha, ha, ha, heh, heh, heh carried across the lobby of London's posh Dorchester Hotel. To me there was little to ha ha or heh heh about, but every simple statement seemed to provoke furious laughter and made him sink deeper into his chair, sending his short legs into the air, only to land a little while later on the ground with a resounding thud.

My cousin's benefactor joined him every time he laughed while I sat there embarrassed by tens of staring eyes questioning this raucousness and recommending a gigglectomy.

I forgot about other people and caught the bug. At one point I got carried away and was at it (for reasons impossible to explain) for over a minute. When I came to, my cousin and his friend were staring at me. I had overdone it. They knew how much these laughter-provoking statements deserved in terms of ha ha, heh heh response and I didn't.

Colonel Muammer Qaddafi's intermediaries are, with one exception, corrupt revolutionaries like himself. They are Palestinians who preach the overthrow of all other Middle Eastern governments because they are not anti-Israeli and anti-Western enough. Their services to Qaddafi consist of schemes to undermine and destabilise his enemies and to support revolutionary movements which promised added support in that direction. Neither our friend in Dubai, nor Prince Mohamad's wandering primitives would do. What is needed here is a bookshelf revolutionary, one keener on lining his pockets than in social change.

This equality principle applies also to dealings with the company, more precisely the company executive who decides with whom to co-operate. We have already dealt with ways to capture a company so this is strictly a comment on the personal factor.

My cousin Fuad Abu Zayad who lives in Kuwait does exceptionally well with major US corporations. Fuad is a Harvard-educated lawyer with a facility to cut across wasteful minutiae and identify the possible. US corporations, limited by restrictive laws and worried about making mistakes, willingly place themselves in his hands to the benefit of both sides. In this case the companies are dealing with the type of man they use in the US.

The haughty representatives of major oil companies cannot deal with Prince Mohamad's crude emissaries. It is difficult for them to communicate. On the other hand, Mohamad's men find kindred spirits in Canadian oil men, themselves an identifiable rough breed. It is amusing to see such types together; their commitment to colourful shirts is one of the more obvious bonds between them.

A Lebanese intermediary is more likely to succeed with a French company. Not only do the Lebanese speak French (Lebanon having been a French colony) but many of them are Roman Catholics and view some Moslem practices with the same undeserved disdain. Nearer the surface of things, the Lebanese and French are alike in their slipperiness and their tendency to stab one in the back. They are equal in their perfidy towards many Middle East notables.

Let's have a close look at my own record.

My favourite and closest associate of all time was Dr Ramzi A. Dalloul who operated in Iraq with considerable success. Ramzi had no interest in wine or women but in power. When not talking about a specific deal we discussed topics ranging from the application of the computer in developing countries to the merits of introducing the Hebrew language in Arab universities. Ramzi and I had gone to school together and we worked together because we liked each other. In a way we were equal.

Mazen Pharoan, a highly influential Saudi businessman, was also one of my classmates. He was not intellectual like Ramzi, but dealt with everyone in a no-nonsense way, without pretence. Mazen excluded me from girly parties because he knew I didn't enjoy them. On the other hand, he once listened to me for two hours then stared me right in the eye with, 'Bullshit . . . I can't dismiss people because they are slightly dishonest or not very bright. They do well here.' I hold a soft spot for his very practical ways.

Our combination of studious inclinations and a preference for truthful behaviour dictated the type of company with which we co-operated. The list includes British Aerospace and George Wimpey from the UK, MAN of West Germany (Ferostal), Société Nouvelle Jossermoz in France, Lott Construction in the US and Ericsson in Sweden. All of these companies are big and businesslike with management groups which are above reproach and distinctly uninterested in being entertained or bribed.

So like calls to like, and intermediaries waste no opportunity of reminding their masters about what brought them together. If an intermediary captures a prince because of their common love for Arabic poetry, he is likely to conduct recitals even when they are not called for. Qaddafi's men talk revolution all the time, while people working with Saudi princes tend to harp on the attractions of Araby's tribal qualities.

Time magazine correspondent Wilton Wynn once described my friend Miles Copeland, an old CIA hand, as the only man who ever used the CIA for cover. The job of the intermediary is indeed his cover.

15

• • •

Conclusions and Projections

The Arab Middle East will, for the foreseeable future, continue to play a central role in global affairs. Its geography and oil make it one of the most strategically important regions in the world. Pressures from within and outside will perpetuate today's instability, with its attendant danger of revolutions, local wars and superpower confrontations.

There are four major forces shaping the destiny of the area. They are intrinsic and will remain the same. They are:

1. The deterioration of social cohesion brought about by sudden wealth and the resultant struggle between haves and have-nots.
2. The Arab–Israeli conflict in general and the issue of Jerusalem in particular.
3. The confrontation between Russia and the West and the rising importance of oil.
4. The Islamic resurgence and its conflict with modern systems of government.

There are many lesser influences, lasting and transitory. Some, like the possibility of Arab unity, are constant factors while others like Palestinian versus Jordanian or Egypt versus Libya are subsidiary issues which appear and disappear leaving faint traces.

The alignments are endlessly variable. There can be no single, clear picture as to where Araby is going. Plausible scenarios abound but exact predictions are foolish and perilous. My

143

conclusions, therefore, about the Arab Middle East and doing business there are general, dealing with unchangeable fundamentals, and are not answers to specific problems. They are simply a basis for an understanding of what is going on in the world's number one hot spot.

The social disruption will continue and will create internal turmoil. Oil wealth has destroyed the old social system of family and tribe and its traditions, including the democratic one of the Bedouin society where a pauper addressed his chief, often a king, by his first name because they were equal in the eyes of Allah. Money has touched every corner of individual, family, tribal and governmental life. Superficially everybody appears happy because they have money. There is no joy, no reason, no love. Teenage sons and daughters listen to the Rolling Stones and Gary Glitter on one radio while their fathers heed the call to prayer on another. Minor tribes have surpassed major ones because they live in territories where oil has been discovered. The business of governing with justice for all has, in some countries, been reduced to money for all. The answer to every complaint is to buy the protesting party. This has submerged the sense of right and wrong in a sea of ready cash.

Swift as the destruction of values and relationships has been their replacement by other workable ones is more difficult and will take generations to effect. It is true that the Koran contains an elaborate social system but, in the absence of a church hierarchy to interpret and adapt its teachings, it cannot cope with the problems of our time.

Today's Arabs have a common language and tradition but they no longer subscribe to the same way of life. All one has to do is walk the streets of Jeddah or Kuwait to encounter creatures of the seventeenth, eighteenth and nineteenth centuries, products of Stone Age feudalism, then walk into a bank and be confronted with a manager who belongs completely to the latter part of the twentieth century. Yet they all do, and must, live together.

The pace of change, and the oil-induced blossoming of a materialistic approach to life are fiercely contested by the traditionalist, too-much-too-soon lobby. These people are perplexed and resentful, full of doubt and therefore afraid. Their opponents say change is the way of the world and are dazzled and bewildered by it, while a minority among them have truly gone Western and are totally alienated from their roots. To explain the Middle East sociologically, a dramatic multiple would have to be applied to the Western notion of a generation gap – and this gap is widening. Much more trouble is on the way with the resurgence of Islam, which, like it or not, appears to be the wave of the future.

The Arab–Israeli conflict will be with us for a long time to come, in spite of Camp David or other peace treaties which might be signed. I am convinced that basic issues such as regional supremacy, or who runs the Middle East, are beyond the scope of such treaties. Furthermore, agreements on Jerusalem, if they come about, will be swept away by the tide of Islamic revival – unless the Arabs get their way, which the Israelis won't allow.

All Arabs feel that the Middle East belongs to them, and that the Israelis are intruders in a political and religious sense. These problems are bigger than the narrow territorial claims of the Palestinians because they involve all Arabs and because they haven't been addressed and both sides pretend they don't exist. Israeli pronouncements about deputising for the West and occupying the oilfields to protect them are stupid and unrealistic and they have pushed this issue to the fore to the delight of Arab radicals and the chagrin of moderates.

Jerusalem and its control appear to present an insoluble difficulty. Not only is it holy to both sides but the holy places physically occupy the same land. A spirit of exceptional moderation would have to prevail on both sides to overcome this thorny problem. President Sadat's failure to secure Israeli co-operation on this issue has produced stubborn reiterations of rigid positions. The antagonists are so far apart no one is trying any more.

Even pro-West Saudi Arabia finds itself the prisoner of its own rhetoric and makes declarations leaving it no room for manoeuvre. Arabs and Moslems of every political shade have adopted the Jerusalem issue. Even faraway Indonesia toes the Moslem line and once haughty, Western-looking Turkey – in need of Saudi funds – plays the same game.

Before there could be a constructive dialogue, Israeli military strength would have to be reduced to equal that of its Arab neighbours. Israel justifies its ability to dictate militarily with its claim to represent the West and its unyielding stance on

Jerusalem. Military parity would restore Arab pride and make the Israelis more reasonable. On the other hand, the Arabs have convinced themselves that Israel's present economic difficulties will lead to its disintegration as a nation state. Certainly, its inability to be self-supporting and its dependence on the US and Jewish organisations for support make it vulnerable, but anticipation of its total disappearnce is simply wishful thinking.

Since military equality and the full recovery of the Israeli economy aren't in the offing, both sides will stick to their guns on the issues of regional supremacy and Jerusalem. Both problems will continue to produce trouble.

Oil wealth and strategic position prevent the possibility of a neutral Middle East. Arabs desire neither to be pawns in the hands of others nor to be taken for granted. But in contrast to their policy on neutrals such as Austria or Finland, the superpowers refuse to leave the Middle East alone. The West rightly cites dependence on oil and other strategic factors as reasons for this attitude. To leave the Middle East alone is to gamble with the West's industrial future, something no Western leader can contemplate.

Russia is projected to need Middle East oil as soon as 1987. This, coupled with the region's vulnerability because of social unrest and strained relations with the West over Israel, will make it hard for Russia to resist taking a plunge into an area that could represent the balance of world power.

The opportunities are wide open for direct or indirect Russian intervention. They could attempt to dismember one of the multi-ethnic states such as Iran or Iraq. They could align themselves openly and aggressively with a radical state like Syria or even the PLO. If such avenues are closed to Russia, and the West refuses to meet her oil needs, she may opt for military intervention and World War Three could result.

The Arabs fear the superpowers not only in terms of conflict but also in terms of possible collusion at their expense. An accommodation between Russia and the US leading to an imposed reduction in or freeze on the price of oil and its allocation, is a prospect that haunts them. The intentions of both the Soviets and the democracies are suspect; the benefit to their economies, and to the world, of an agreement to share the oil wealth of the Middle East would be huge.

Alternatives to oil as an energy source are in the distant future. In addition, an effective détente in Europe has enhanced the strategic importance of the Middle East. The pressure on the Arabs to lean East or West will continue to bring about dangerous confrontations. Erratic as they are, the Arabs have masterfully kept both sides at bay – so far.

The Islamic resurgence and the desire to shut out the 'morally corrupt' world of Western Christendom and revert to traditional socio-religious values is one of the major political movements of our time.

Sporadic flirtations with Russia by Egypt, Syria, Iraq, Libya, South Yemen and others have failed. They have all signed treaties and bought arms when it suited them. Based on a game of power politics rather than ideology, such alliances come unstuck at the first hint of conflicting interests. Contrary to the common Western belief that the Russians prostitute themselves to gain favour with the Arabs, Russia has been tough in its denials of the supply of modern weapons and economic aid, and demands hard currency payments even from its closest 'ally', Syria. A change in policy on both issues is always possible.

The West continues to be viewed as an economic exploiter. Even the West's staunchest Arab allies subscribe to this theory. In Saudi Arabia, oil minister Sheikh Yamani is extremely unpopular with the young for his public position on the protection of Western economic health and his advocacy of a sensible policy to moderate price increases. In some countries the immediate past is colonialism, and that rankles. Thirdly, there is the West's unmistakable lack of understanding of Islam, which they link to words like duplicity, cruelty, servility and despotism. With Jerusalem as a backdrop, these factors augur against smooth relations between the Arabs and the West.

Nasser's experiment with Arab unity was the most serious one. It – with others – is in ruins; tribalism and regionalism won. Arab empires of the past were held together by Islam; religion and the state were one and the same. When the two were split by 'progressive' political thinking, the absence of an equivalent force proved fatal and imported political ideology proved unpalatable for the masses. This has led the area back to its single common denominator: Islam.

Religion has always been there, just below the surface. Saudi Arabia's constitution is the Koran and the country is a theocracy. Even modern heads of state, like King Hussein of Jordan and President Mubarak of Egypt, appeal to the faithful by having their pictures in reverent poses appear in newspapers. The man in the street can't go too many sentences without praising Allah the merciful and benevolent – even when poor or sick or hungry.

Islam has resurfaced as a political force because the alternatives have failed. The West is seen as exploitative, the anti-religious nature of Soviet ideology is inimical, and the call for Arab unity, on geographical and social grounds, went largely unanswered. Islam, by contrast, stirs every dormant dream in the Arab historcal mind. The vision of a strong Islamic empire appeals to all, including the boozers and womanisers.

The modern Islamic movement is admirable for its high, puritan ideals, but it is inefficient and intolerant. The proposed Islamic form of government by Khomeini, the Moslem Brotherhood and other advocates of Islamic fundamentalism lacks the machinery to cope with twentieth-century problems. Not only would it not allow for dissent but it would stifle healthy change. Both unbelievers and non-believers would suffer, organised government would give way to the inexactitude of Koran interpreters and would collapse, and relations with the outside world would be strained for lack of ability to communicate with the twentieth century. The absence of a church hierarchy to assimilate the teachings of the Koran in today's world is catastrophic and even if one were created, progress would be slow against people's adherence to the word which descended from heaven and cannot be tampered with. Besides, the Koran has lain untouched for centuries. The required change is too drastic to be absorbed at once.

A reversion to Islam has begun all over the Middle East. Kings and rulers who would be adversely affected by its success pay it lip service because they can't go against the good book. They seek accommodation instead of confrontation. The hope of stopping this reversion is very faint, and lies only in the possible failure of its early applications, such as in Khomeini's Iran. The spread of the Islamic movement will lead to antiquated systems of government, loss of liberty and more turmoil. Dark days are ahead.

Amidst all this discontent and strife, there are some – if few –

positive elements to celebrate: Arabism has survived the failure of Nasser's grand attempt at unity, and other feeble ones. As a result significant grass-roots developments have taken place.

Dialects are disappearing because people travel more and listen to each other's radio stations. This will help bring Arabic up to date and give it a chance to assimiliate foreign technological words. It also helps create a central pool of human talent, which the Middle East desperately needs.

Associations for Arab doctors, engineers, lawyers, etc. are in existence and effective. Work in these fields is gradually becoming standardised, and this has contributed more to real Arab unity than any recent political movements.

The rich countries (Saudi Arabia, Kuwait, etc.) are sharing their wealth with poor ones (Egypt, Syria, Jordan, et al) and oil wealth is filtering through to simple Mohamads, Alis and Abdullahs. This has kicked Communism in the ideological teeth, leaving it with little mass appeal. But it has resurrected a new sense of power whose natural base is Islam.

It is against this sociological, economic and political background that the intermediary and skimmer operate. Will they be with us in the future? The answer is yes.

We have shown an absence of social cohesion, a governmental system in painful transition, outside influences undeterred by the damage they cause and an angry Islamic movement trying to reassert itself and make sense through reimposition of old, unsuitable values.

We are dealing with a race that believes in Allah and in individual genius, in the man rather than the form of government. The head of state rules as well as reigns and countries and their policies reflect his will.

The Arab Middle East is run by men, not institutions. In the absence of established self-perpetuating institutions the men who rule praise Allah and depend on other men they trust, who in turn depend on others, and so it goes down the line. This is an extension of the tribal system and this is where intermediaries and skimmers live. They are not an accident but an expression of a slow-changing tradition which rewards loyalty and regards it more highly than competence. Anyone who suggests that King Fahd of Saudi Arabia is unaware of the doings of his brother Prince Sultan, or

President Saddam Hussein of the funny dealings of his generals, is a fool. Both sides are taking care of their own and their own take care of them. These men are protecting their power base.

Judged by Western values, honest men exist here even today and will be part of the Middle East of the future. They are Western in outlook and their attitude is a combination of borrowed morality, and anger at the excesses of the present system. The idea of giving and receiving is part and parcel of Arab history. Wealth of unknown dimensions has focused attention on it and it no longer serves as a traditional distribution system, but has produced gross abuses. Wealth has corrupted an otherwise usable system. More of it will cause more social disruption and mental imbalance. (An Arab does not speak of drinking but of getting drunk.)

As long as the Middle East is men dealing with men, whatever change takes place will be minimal and buying people's loyalties will still be with us. I do not believe Western values can prevail in the Middle East. Modern Arabs will have to evolve their own values, and this will take time. Inevitably they will incorporate an Islamic outlook blunted by Western ideas and able to accommodate the age of electronic communications.

I believe that the intermediary system is wholly necessary in Middle Eastern business dealings. Sadly, oil and the Arab temperament have pushed things too far. But the intermediary cannot be ignored. He is here to stay.